Through Peking's Sewer Gate

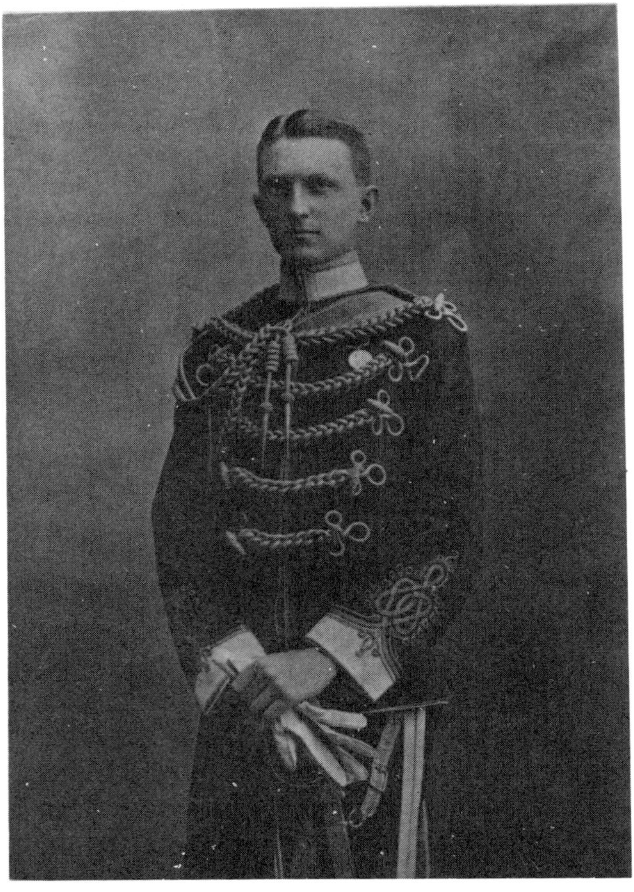

THROUGH PEKING'S SEWER GATE

RELIEF OF THE BOXER SIEGE, 1900–1901

Richard A. Steel

Edited and with an Introduction by
George W. Carrington

VANTAGE PRESS
New York / Washington / Atlanta
Los Angeles / Chicago

To soldiers, sailors, and marines

FIRST EDITION

All rights reserved, including the right of
reproduction in whole or in part in any form.

Copyright © 1985 by George Williams Carrington

Published by Vantage Press, Inc.
516 West 34th Street, New York, New York 10001

Manufactured in the United States of America
ISBN: 533-06126-1

Library of Congress Catalog Card No.: 84-90046

CONTENTS

Illustrations — vii
Foreword, by Sir Colin Crowe — ix
Editor's Preface — xi
Introduction — xiii

1. Arrival in China, July 15–26, 1900 — 1

2. The Move from the Taku Forts to Tientsin,
   July 27–August 3, 1900 — 6

3. The Military Attack from Tientsin to Peking,
   August 4–14, 1900 — 13

4. Consolidation of Peking, Looting, and Chasing the Boxers,
   August 15–September 28, 1900 — 54

5. A Trip Out to Other Parts of China,
   September 29–November 20, 1900 — 68

6. A Winter in Garrison in Peking and the Summer Palace,
   November 21, 1900–March 27, 1901 — 75

7. Lieutenant Steel Departs from China,
   March 28–April 28, 1901 — 95

ILLUSTRATIONS

MAPS

The Taku Forts	4
Tientsin to Peking	14
Allied Approach to Peking; the Legations	27
Peking	54

DOCUMENTS

Field Message, 4 August 1900	15
Last Page of Letter Lieutenant Steel Wrote to His Uncle, with Sketch of Peking	26
Queen Victoria Military Funeral Service Order, January 30, 1901	85
Regulations for Visitors to the Summer Palace	96

PHOTOGRAPHS

The International Force

Plate 1. Japanese Infantry	28
Plate 2. U.S. Troops	29
Plate 3. Punjabi Infantry	29
Plate 4. Australian Contingent	30
Plate 5. Allied Troops	30
Plate 6. Italian Officers	31
Plate 7. French Transport	31
Plate 8. German Four-in-Hand Brake	32

Military Operations
   Plate 9. R.I.M.S. *Dalhousie* . . . 33
   Plate 10. Taku North Fort . . . 33
   Plate 11. The Sewer Gate . . . 34
   Plate 12. Bamboo Ramp . . . 34
   Plate 13. Ruins . . . 35
   Plate 14. Breach in Wall . . . 35
   Plate 15. "Puffing Billy" . . . 36
   Plate 16. Curios . . . 36

Officials and Individuals
   Plate 17. Li Hung-chang . . . 37
   Plate 18. Lt. Cdr. Roger Keyes . . . 38
   Plate 19. Gen. Sir Alfred Gaselee . . . 39
   Plate 20. Field Marshal Count von Waldersee . . . 40
   Plate 21. Gen. O'Moore Creagh . . . 40
   Plate 22. Chinese Servant and Dog . . . 41
   Plate 23. Maj. T. E. Scott . . . 42
   Plate 24. General Barrow . . . 43

The Chinese
   Plate 25. Wood Sawyers . . . 44
   Plate 26. A Barber . . . 45
   Plate 27. Neighbors . . . 46
   Plate 28. Workers . . . 46
   Plate 29. A Funeral . . . 47
   Plate 30. A Storyteller . . . 47
   Plate 31. Prisoners . . . 48
   Plate 32. A Peking Cart . . . 48

The City of Peking
   Plate 33. Drum Tower . . . 49
   Plate 34. Pei T'ang Cathedral . . . 50
   Plate 35. Coal Hill . . . 50
   Plate 36. Lama Temple . . . 51
   Plate 37. The Tsungli Yamen . . . 51
   Plate 38. Forbidden City . . . 52
   Plate 39. Marble Boat . . . 52
   Plate 40. Throne of China . . . 53

FOREWORD

The difference between the world of 1900 and that of today in its political, social, and military circumstances is as great, and probably greater, than between the beginning and end of any period of similar length in history. Nowhere is this gulf greater than between the China of 1900 and that of 1984. It is a gulf not only of circumstances, but of comprehension. The China, and particularly the Peking, of the years before the Japanese War is a vanished world. For non-Chinese in China, the century between 1840 and 1940 was an extraordinary period. The life they lived in Peking and the treaty ports was unique to such an extent as to be incomprehensible to those who did not experience it. Those who did are a small and diminishing group. For the sake of history, it is important that all records, and particularly personal records, of the time be preserved and published.

This is why the diary of Lieutenant Steel is a valuable document and why it is good that it should be published. Admittedly, it reveals no new historical facts. It shows no insight into the nature of Chinese society or government; it was not meant to. It was not written for publication, but is a straightforward account of what a British subaltern did every day during the expedition for the relief of the legations in Peking from the siege in 1900 and the subsequent occupation of the city by foreign troops.

Lieutenant Steel was a regular army officer of the period. He was not writing his memoirs, and he did not confide his opinions to his diary. But he was immensely meticulous—for example, in the way he recorded on the blank blotting paper that was interleaved between each page of the diary the letters he wrote and the letters he received. He made one or two sketches there, which show he could draw and had a perceptive eye. He also showed his eye in the photographs he took and developed himself (no mean feat in those days) and in the government photographs he collected, which together are the best collection I have seen of old Peking and reproduce its former winter-time atmosphere, clear yet dust-laden, brilliantly. And his remark of the Forbidden City that "the actual buildings . . . are grass-grown and have the indescribable appearance of combined splendour and neglect so common to Chinese palaces" is exactly right.

Finally, the diary is also of great interest in the indirect light it throws on the widespread extent of British power in 1900—for the Boer War was going on at the time—and how much Britain depended on Indian military. Nearly all the British troops on the relief march described by Lieutenant Steel were Indians, Sikhs, Rajputs, Punjabis, or Bengal Lancers, and the whole expedition was mounted from India.

Colonel Carrington is to be congratulated on the way he has edited and faithfully reproduced the diary and set it in the context in which it was written. We are much in his debt.

Sir Colin Crowe
United Kingdom Permanent
Representative to the United Nations
1970–73

EDITOR'S PREFACE

Two journals, covering the years 1900 and 1901, were dutifully completed by a twenty-six-year-old British army officer, Richard A. Steel. They were made available for editing and comment, along with the photographs that are included in this work, by his son, Greville Steel.

The entries from July 15, 1900, to April 28, 1901, comprising Lieutenant Steel's adventure as aide-de-camp to Gen. Alfred Gaselee, commanding the British contingent of the allied relief expedition to Peking (Plate 19), constitute the narrative.

Substantial editorial comment on the historical and contemporary events bearing on the Boxer uprising and the siege of the Peking legations is certainly necessary, however, to explain the background for the diary of this young officer. I hopefully contend that a most interesting aspect of this book is the contrast that it presents between the personal preoccupations, experiences, and attitudes of a Victorian-Age officer coming precipitously from India to China as a member of an international punitive expedition and the violent and chaotic conditions in North China and Peking incident to the crumbling of a decadent Manchu dynasty unable any longer to sustain traditional patterns of Chinese society against the onslaught of foreign intruders.

Since diaries are chronological, they usually do not allow separation into chapters. In the present case, however, it is logical to think of Lieutenant Steel's adventure in segments—his arrival in China, preparations for combat, the attack from Tientsin to Peking, the mopping-up and looting of Peking, a trip out to other cities of China, winter garrison duty, and his departure from China. This, then, is the basis for arrangement of this diary into chapters. The editor's preliminary comments also roughly parallel this division of material.

Corrections or alterations have been made to the grammar, spellings, and capitalization of the original. Military ranks, identifications, affiliations, and diplomatic titles were important to the author and his age, so they have been reproduced in full in order to standardize and to avoid the confusion of incomprehensible abbreviations. Victorian usage was to capitalize in some references that which would be now lower-cased. The editor follows the earlier practice. Lieutenant Steel's original diary accounted for every day of his stay in China. The uneventful days, however, have been omitted in this volume. Every month, the diary heading reminds of the arrival of a new month.

The photographs have been taken from Steel's personal album. Some few of those reproduced were official photographs and are so designated, but the great majority were taken and developed by the diarist.

One cannot help but notice how little he experienced of China itself or of its people. He was only a transient foreigner on the scene. This is a part of the very contrast between his observations and my comments on the tragedy and importance of these months of Chinese history.

Lieutenant Steel was the father of two sons. The elder was Sir Christopher Steel, G.C.M.G., M.V.O., who was British ambassador to West Germany from 1957 to 1963. The younger was Col. Richard Greville Acton Steel, T.D., who received the U.S. Bronze Star Medal for service with the U.S. First Army in 1944–45. He lived in the Cotswolds, indulging in those enthusiasms of a Steel, fishing and shooting. In a generous act of loyalty and trust, he made his father's diary and photographs available to me, also an enthusiast of the Cotswolds, a student of China, and a military veteran of a postwar period of turmoil in Peking.

INTRODUCTION

Richard Alexander Steel in India

Richard Alexander Steel was born in 1874 in India. As the son of a colonel, he quite naturally aspired for and achieved a career of his own in the army. He kept a diary of his military career over many years. The segment before us covers his experiences from July 1900 to April 1901 in China, when and where he accompanied, as aide-de-camp, Gen. Sir Alfred Gaselee, the commander of the British contingent of the allied relief expedition to raise the Boxer siege of the Peking legations (Plate 19). The contingent was termed by the British themselves the China Field Force.

Steel returned from India to England for his education at Rugby School and the Royal Military College, Sandhurst. Upon graduation from that training institution, he intended to join the Indian army, but having put his name down for the cavalry, he found himself gazetted a second lieutenant with the Seventh Dragoon Guards. He could not afford this assignment, but indeed eventually managed a career as a cavalryman.

The lieutenant obtained a transfer to the Irish Fusiliers in Egypt. He later obtained another transfer to the Seventeenth (Indian) Bengal Lancers, the name of which was later changed to Seventeenth Cavalry. He saw active service on the northwest frontier of India and on the Mohmand expedition of 1897 under General Elles. This punitive expedition to subdue the Afghan

Mohmands, who had for years persistently raided British territory, constituted Lieutenant Steel's combat experience prior to the march of the international allied relief expedition on August 14, 1900, from Tientsin to Peking.

He was notified of his appointment as aide-de-camp to the viceroy of India, Lord Curzon of Kedleston, on January 23, 1900. His diary noted: "Got wire from Mil. Sec.: Viceroy asking if I would like to go as extra A.D.C. Replied 'Yes.' " Curzon's achievements as governor-general of India, chancellor of Oxford, and foreign minister lay largely before him in 1900, but he had already travelled in Central Asia, Persia, Afghanistan, Siam, Indochina, and Korea. He was an influential mentor for Lieutenant Steel and generously consented to his aide's participation in the adventure of China. Rumors of trouble from the Boxers had reached India, although they had not come prominently to Lieutenant Steel's attention, judging from the lack of any comment in his diary. On June 20, 1900, he heard from the viceroy that "General Gaselee was to command the China Expedition." The next day, "I went round and asked to go as Orderly Officer to General Gaselee and after lunch heard to my delight that I had got it. Dinner and dance at Viceregal Lodge, and many congratulations on my good luck."

Lieutenant Steel's diary account is a *social* commentary on the duties, diversions, and experiences of a subaltern in India and China in 1900. It also constitutes a *political* report on China, with revelations on the attitudes and conduct of foreigners towards the crumbling Ch'ing dynasty of the Manchus, dominated by Boxers crazed with hatred of these foreigners. Finally, the diary is a *military* account of the march to Peking and the subsequent garrisoning of China's capital by an international force.

His diary over his months of service in India constituted, quite naturally, entries on the pleasurable aspects of his life. In garrison—that is to say, in peacetime—a soldier had to work hard at his diversions, play, parties, friends, and athletics.

Steel, as an aide, had no duties with troops. His references to any military obligations or preoccupations were limited to revolver practice, parades, riding, polo, gymkhana, tent pegging, chasing rabbits, exercising horses, tilting, paper chase competitions, race-course meetings, torchlight tattoos, and language study of Pushtoo. A soldier's life in camp was and is boring. In any case, the noncommissioned officers were available to train, discipline, and handle the native Indian cavalry, infantry, and artillery troops destined to embark from Calcutta in July 1900 for China.

But the young officer had a well-developed social life that must have expanded even further when he became aide to the viceroy. There were trips out of Calcutta—to Kalka, Simla, Allahabad, Barrackpore, Cawnpore, Quetta, Kohat, Dinapore, Amritsar, and Lahore.

He attended or visited fancy dress balls, a levee in full dress, garden parties, "at homes," picnics, dinners, teas, luncheons, banquets, church services, dances, theatres, plays, shows, horse and dog shows, museums, the zoo, races, concerts, recitals, musicales, audiences, funerals, festivals, homes, hotels, and bungalows. He also visited the U.S. Institution of India, the Mohammedan Literary Society, the Eurasian Society, art schools, and a carpet factory.

He maintained a loyal, regular correspondence with many friends and relatives. He was careful in his handling and payment of his servants, grooms, and bearers—one of whom, the faithful Algoo, was to serve him for over three years and accompany him to China. Steel walked for pleasure and for exercise, drove in many types of carriages, enjoyed use of the viceroy's launch on the Hooghly River at Calcutta, read, sketched, enjoyed his dogs, fished, and hunted everything from birds to tigers.

He attended or viewed a biograph, which one learns is a cinematograph, or machine for projecting a series of pictures giving an illusion of continuous action. In India, he took photos, and we can be grateful for his growing interest in photography. Later, in Hong Kong he bought a "Kodak," and in Peking he took and developed himself the photographs that illustrate this diary.

Athletics, of course, were important in the young lieutenant's life. He rode bicycles as well as horses. He played golf, tennis, racquets, billiards, and football. It is surprising that he never wrote of playing cricket. A favorite pastime was a game "in 'sticky' court with the marker," which sounds perhaps like squash.

Lieutenant Steel was twenty-six in the late spring of 1900. His land of birth and the arena of his military career, India, delimited his social, athletic, and intellectual horizons. It is not to disparage his education and his consciousness of outside world events to say that the news of a crisis in China must have come as a complete surprise. He was probably a very typical, gentleman officer in Victorian India. His diary made no mention of world events; nor did it contain any observations on politics. Who were Boxers? Where was Peking?

He embarked on July 4, 1900, in the Hooghly at Calcutta, bound for combat in a country about which he apparently knew nothing. He sailed on the *Lebenghla,* originally employed in shipping to New Zealand, with Captain Pell, another aide; his fellow officers; his troops (largely native Indians); his horses, mules, and ponies; and his "kit"—the material for combat. The *Lebenghla* was "not well fitted in her present condition for transport of troops, especially in hot climates." She was accompanied by another ship, the *Itinda*. They arrived in Hong Kong in two weeks.

Chinese Antiforeignism and the Boxer Movement

Before we follow Lieutenant Steel, General Gaselee, the British contingent, and, for that matter, the thousands of other foreign troops from several nations onward to Tientsin and Peking, the causes for their presence should be examined.

A start may be made with China's traditional historic concept of world society. China considered itself the center of the world, rejecting ideas of juridical equality among nation states, preferring seclusion and only deigning to accept trifling, superficial trade with the foreigners on the mudflats at Canton under an old framework of tribute submission. China felt herself to be self-sufficient, in no need of the goods of the "barbarians" or of their presence.

The foreigners, however, eager for the fabled exports of China and having no products of value needed by China to exchange for silk, tea, artifacts, and other treasures, paid in silver. Eventually, however, they hit upon opium as an item to be peddled for profit, and the drug was employed to enslave Chinese masses in misery and to reverse the flow of silver back out of China.

Although the first Westerners to visit China held a high regard for Chinese culture, history, and achievements, the complications of the opium trade and the military confrontations of the nineteenth century caused a deterioration of this regard into an attitude of disdain and scorn. They regarded the Chinese as static and decadent heathen, a mass of dirty coolies who preferred seclusion and affected an unjustifiable racial superiority. The Chinese, in turn, returning the compliment, saw the Westerners affecting racial antipathies. The greedy merchants were uncouth "barbarians," with strange faces, weird manners, and grotesque religious tenets.

Consider the course of nineteenth-century relations between China and the West. The first Sino-British War, the Opium War, 1839–42, had resulted in the loss to China of Hong Kong, a large indemnity, and the cession of privileges in the first five treaty ports. The flood of merchants, missionaries, travellers, diplomats, advisers, and reporters to China began. Shanghai and Tientsin, in particular, and concession areas in other cities arose as European-style cities. The customs revenues were placed under the management of the foreigners.

In 1858–60, the foreigners, forcing recognition of their "rights" upon the emperor, marched to Peking, destroyed the Summer Palace, and initiated a new set of privileges for trade in more treaty ports. Britain secured a new lease on Kowloon. Russia acquired a new domain on the Amur River at China's expense, the Far East Maritime Provinces. France concentrated on a new empire in Indochina, traditionally tributary to China, and forced new concessions in behalf of Roman Catholic missionaries. Japan temporarily occupied southern Taiwan in 1874, incorporated the Ryūkyū (Liu-Ch'iu) Islands, and led the way in forcing the Manchu emperor to receive the foreign envoys in person. Russia bit off more Chinese territory in Turkestan. Britain incorporated Lower and Upper Burma.

In 1894, the dismemberment of China accelerated. Japan surprised the world with an easy victory over China, this time retaining Taiwan and the Pescadores and ensuring a Korea independent of China. Germany, late to achieve unified nationhood, hurried now to carve out its own sphere of influence. The murder of two German missionaries in Shantung provided the kaiser with a superficial excuse to occupy Kiaochow Bay and Tsingtao, ordering the Chinese to withdraw from their own territory. Such decisive moves were regarded by other Europeans as intelligent diplomacy, cutting through the necessity of long negotiations that they had had to endure. But China was touchy about Shantung, the province of Confucius and home of larger-than-normal, strong, aggressive, and proud Chinese. A resistance movement, antagonistic particularly to the Germans, began in Shantung under the lead of the Society of the Righteous Fist, the Boxers.

If the Germans were to have Kiaochow Bay, the Russians, in turn, insisted upon their exclusive rights in Port Arthur and Dairen, as extensions of their ambitions to dominate Manchuria through railroad rights. In turn, Britain demanded and got a new base in Weihaiwei in Shantung, where Lieutenant Steel, in the *Lebenghla,* called on his way to the Taku forts (Plate 10), Tientsin, and Peking, France obtained new rights in Kwangchouwan in the south. Only the Italians, testing the water in Chekiang Province, were resisted by China. Could this have been the first, symbolic change in the long, hard, humiliating process of China's dismemberment? No wonder the time was ripe for some group such as the Boxers.

One need not look beyond this physical dismemberment of China for sufficient cause for antiforeignism, but think also of what accompanied these moves that had made the Yangtze Valley British; Manchuria, Russian; Shantung, German; Taiwan and Fukien, Japanese; and Yunnan, Kweichow, and Kwangsi, French. Foreign goods, methods, controls, ideologies, and renegade criminals were penetrating into all parts of proud China. New railroads, exploitation of the mines, the opening of trading stations and companies, and domination of China's overland and riverine routes of communication did little for China's needs, merely upsetting old economic patterns and throwing coolie thousands out of work. Riots, burnings, destruction of property, and demonstrations against the economic penetrations of the foreigners became frequent in the 1880s and 1890s. These necessitated suppression and reparations to the injured foreigners. The Europeans were secluded, privileged, arrogant, and protected by the treaty rights guaranteed by the system of extraterritoriality.

The most dramatic manifestation of Chinese antiforeignism, however, was to be seen in the antimissionary movement. Innocent Europeans in their homelands would least understand this, but in China itself the missionary presence and activities came to represent the Boxers' foremost protest and target. Despite their good works, the missionaries were viewed by antiforeign elements as living secluded and privileged lives and being arrogant, presumptuous, and intolerant about the Chinese's own tenets in an ancient, cultured, and pragmatic society.

The missionaries asserted unwarranted privileges for their converts. They themselves were sheltered in special homes and compounds. A scurrilous, false body of anti-Christian literature grew in the 1890s, feeding upon other faults and failings of the foreigners, but mostly maligning the missionaries and their practices. Resort was made to name-calling. The literary attack upon Christian missionaries utilized ridicule of the missionaries' beliefs and rituals.

Against this background of basic, mutual antipathy between Chinese and foreigner, the dismemberment of China by the international powers, the penetration of economic China, and the antiforeignism, particularly to be observed in the antimissionary movement, many Chinese sought answers from a traditional source in times of trouble, the secret society. Secret societies were ancient in China. There had been the Triads, the White Lotus, Eight Diagrams, Red Fists, Big Knives, and Big Sword societies. Now there arose, particularly in Shantung, the Society of Harmonious Fists, the Boxers. They offered to Chinese who would listen to them an answer to their troubles.

The Boxers relied upon ritual secrecy, magic, claims of invulnerability, ceremonial show, incantations, flamboyant dress, ornamentation, and weapons to dominate and win their followers. But they could easily point to and blame the foreigners for all of China's misfortunes. The harvest failures, Yellow River floods, locusts, famines, dislocations to work patterns caused by new railroads, and the affronts to the spirits caused by the new foreign telegraph gave them more converts.

Initially, the Manchus themselves worried about the Boxers as an opposition element, but gradually they were perceived by many in Peking as China's answer to the hated Christian foreigners. A sympathetic governor in Shantung, a green light given by the empress dowager herself, and a gradual spread of anarchy allowed the movement to spread and gain new adherents. Demonstrations, riots, and destruction of property were followed by actual killings of Chinese Christian converts. The first white foreign missionary was murdered on December 31, 1899. Recruiting to the Boxer side and the incitement of incidents continued in Chihli in the spring of 1900, frightening missionaries out of the countryside into taking refuge in the cities of Tientsin and Peking.

The siege of the European legations in Peking by the Boxers is generally considered to have commenced on June 20, 1900. The international force had been gathering off Taku Forts to do something about the situation.

Escalation of the Boxer Movement: Events at the Taku Forts and at Tientsin

In Shantung, where the Boxers arose, they were initially perceived as an anti-Manchu force, a threat to the regime. The German colonists spreading into Shantung classified them as bandits. Gradually, however, the prospect of sponsorship by the Manchus and the empress dowager herself became more probable. Scholars have differed over the theory that there might have been a conspiracy all along between the throne and the Boxers, but, in fact, the empress dowager called for militia action against them in 1898. Tz'u-hsi and the Boxers were, in any case, becoming allied in an ever-increasing antiforeign and anti-Christian attitude. The Boxers promised answers to those disaffected by growing antagonism towards the new, foreign-built railways opening up North China. They appealed, as well, to those who suffered from the widespread floods, droughts, and famines, which persisted on the old Yellow River plain in Shantung.

In 1899, Governor Yü-hsien of Shantung, who was intensely antiforeign, favored the Boxers. He allowed them to operate with impunity. The demonstrations, lootings, and attacks on Christian converts grew and spread to neighboring Chihli, the metropolitan province wherein lay Peking. Yü-hsien was succeeded by Governor Yüan Shih-k'ai, who might have suppressed the Boxers. By her equivocal language in an important edict, however, the empress dowager declared that, although she abhorred brigands, she saw nothing wrong with peaceful, law-abiding citizens perfecting their skills in mechanical arts, mutual help, and self-defense. The foreigners in Peking protested this edict, but the empress dowager in effect had expressed her benign approval of the Boxers.

Meanwhile, there had been a fresh burst of Western intrusion into Peking and Tientsin. Christian missionaries, particularly the Welsh Baptist editor and mission worker Timothy Richard, translated Western books, tracts, pamphlets, and suggestions for altering the Chinese state and Chinese life itself. The Kuang-hsü emperor, influenced by K'ang Yu-wei, a modernizer and reformer, ignored the wishes of the empress dowager and boldly issued a series of edicts that would have revolutionized and altered China.

The Hundred Days of Reform were abruptly ended, however, on September 30, 1898, with Yüan Shih-k'ai showing his support for the conservatives, cancellation of the edicts, the removal of the emperor from power, and the execution or sending into exile of the reformers. A result was an increase in antiforeignism in Peking, out of a fear that the foreigners might intervene to restore the emperor to the throne. The several allied powers reacted by bringing in some 115 armed guards to protect the legations and their citizens.

The U.S. and British ministers to China sent warning messages to their governments on the increasing danger to foreigners in North China after the first white missionary had been killed by Boxers on the last day of 1899. Yü-hsien and Prince Tuan, extremists in their antiforeignism, played parts behind the scenes in encouraging pro-Boxer policies. They opposed the influence of moderate Prince Ch'ing, who controlled the Tsungli Yamen, China's Foreign Affairs Office. Jung-lu, the army commander, loyal to the empress dowager, seemed to place himself in the middle of the policy debate.

The foreign diplomats temporarily settled their national differences and suppressed their eccentric personalities to the degree necessary for the composition of a series of identical notes calling for action against the threatening Boxers. A futile diplomatic struggle persisted throughout the spring of 1900, centering over a proclamation to be issued by the throne against the Boxers. Instead, moderate officials were dismissed from their jobs and Yü-hsien was given a new governorship in Shansi. The Europeans began to deploy naval reinforcements to the Bay of Chihli and to deliberate a show of force or the dispatch of even further numbers of legation guards to Peking.

The Boxers concentrated their antagonisms on two so-called "Christian" centers, Paotingfu, a railroad center and missionary base, and Tungchou, another missionary center close to Peking. Skirmishes occurred there and elsewhere in the Chihli countryside. A massacre of Chinese Christian converts at Paotingfu was reported by the Roman Catholic Bishop Favier to the French minister Pichon. The British and Russian ministers, natural leaders of the foreign legations, still were not particularly alarmed over the imminence of true danger. They accepted the reassurances of the Tsungli Yamen that there was no threat to the group of foreigners in the city. In late May, two British missionaries and their converts were murdered northeast of Paotingfu and the foreign ministers announced that they contemplated increasing the numbers of the legation guards.

On May 28, news reached Peking of a second attack on Paotingfu and its railway facilities. The telegraph lines had been cut; the railroad tracks, stations, warehouses, and bridges had been destroyed; and two groups of foreign engineers and their families had been put to rout and cut off. The ministers called up landing parties from their fleet units off the Taku forts. Some 340 poorly equipped additional troops were sent to Peking on May 31 by train. A rescue party led by Auguste Chamot, the Swiss manager of the Peking Hotel, sallied forth to rescue the first group, composed of Belgian railroad engineers. They had, fortunately, evaded any clash with Boxers, but observed that regular Chinese troops, ostensibly sent to defend the foreigners, had joined in the looting of foreign property. The second body of foreigners, however, suffered a frightful ordeal. Some were massacred and their bodies mutilated, and the others struggled, under attack, to reach Tientsin. The survivors told a story that horrified the foreigners and hardened attitudes.

British Minister MacDonald got no satisfaction from his protests to the Tsungli Yamen. The Boxers now turned their attention away from the Paotingfu rail line, running to the southwest of Peking, and turned instead to the direct line to Tientsin, angered at the fact that legation reinforcements had arrived by this route. A Chinese army commander who had defended the line against the Boxers was ordered off, rather than given support. Parleys to negotiate restrictions upon the Boxers' activities failed because they were half-hearted or sham. Whole-scale domination of the countryside by Boxers was a fact. They began to appear in Peking itself. The Peking racecourse, the foreigners' favorite symbolic recreational site, was burned. This impelled Minister MacDonald to request urgently a relief force to be sent to Peking by Vice Adm. Sir Edward Seymour, in command of naval units off the Taku forts.

By June 10, Peking was full of Boxers and fierce, menacing Kansu soldiers from the west. Cannons were being deployed on the high and dominating Ch'ien Men edifice. All telegraph and mail services were cut. Prince Ch'ing and all moderate officials were removed from office. The foreigners organized their barricades and began to lay in stocks of food. A Japanese diplomat, Sugiyama, was murdered while he was returning unarmed from an attempt to meet expected arriving, reinforcing troops.

On June 13, the Boxers began a general attack on all Christian converts, burned all the churches, markets, and stores dealing with foreigners, and first attacked the legations. A patrol of Europeans, finding Boxers holding Chinese Christian prisoners, shot forty-six Boxers. On June 19, the foreigners were given an ultimatum to march out through the hostile countryside, out of Peking, out of China. They feared that such a column, including women and children, would be slaughtered. Their indecision on whether to comply or not was resolved for them by the murder in the open streets of Peking of the German minister von Ketteler, who had endeavored to speak for them to the Tsungli Yamen. They stayed. The siege was underway.

And what about Admiral Seymour and events in Tientsin? The first 340 legation reinforcements had been sent up by rail on May 30 and 31 from some fifteen foreign warships. Further naval units and troops continued to arrive. The progress of events alarmed the admirals. On June 9, Admiral Seymour received Minister MacDonald's request for a relief force.

Seymour immediately landed, without consulting his colleagues, and set out, with no prior planning, to lead a contingent under his personal direction many miles across hostile territory. He had an international force of 2,100 men, almost one-half being British. The advance was to be by rail, but the cars were soon halted by Boxer destruction of the tracks ahead and behind them. The admiral next hoped to relieve Peking by junks, using the Pei Ho river route, but found that Chinese army troops, which he had counted on to forestall the Boxers, had, in fact, joined them in opposing his column.

By June 19, he had abandoned his railway trains, found the river too low for easy junk progress, and been forced to leave behind his heavy weapons and equipment. The harassed group finally attacked and took the Hsiku Arsenal, a large building near Tientsin itself, where they found food, water, and stores. They holed up, to await rescue by Russian troops and escort back to Tientsin on June 26. Instead of effecting a relief of Peking, they themselves had to be rescued and brought in. It was a psychological victory for the antiforeign Chinese, including the Boxers. The next relief column commander could not be a British officer—that is to say, Lieutenant Steel's General Gaselee—but had to be a German (although Field Marshal Count von Waldersee was to be too late in arriving on the scene for the next episode).

The foreign naval commanders off the Taku forts paused before pouring more troops piecemeal after Admiral Seymour. On June 15, the Boxers took control of the walled native city of Tientsin, separate and apart from the Tientsin foreign concessions. There was no news of Admiral Seymour. Now the foreigners in Tientsin believed that they themselves might be put under siege or massacred. Peking's relief was on the conscience of all, but Tientsin itself first had to be made secure.

On June 14, there was a rumor about that the German minister, von Ketteler, had been killed in Peking. On June 16, the European capitals were startled at a news item supposedly confirming von Ketteler's death. Von Ketteler was killed, however, on June *20*. The news and telegraph agencies involved might have been favored before the fact with advance information on only an intended victim.

The Boxer occupation of Tientsin city and the von Ketteler rumor, although it was of a deed only later to eventuate, probably were the factors that determined the admirals under their senior, the Russian admiral Alexeiev, governor-general of Port Arthur, to occupy the Taku forts. They had to secure Tientsin and the Pei Ho line of communications north. They did not want full-scale war. They asserted that their intended action was being taken in order to maintain contact with forces already ashore and to uphold order. They pointed out that the Chinese army was already acting in collaboration with the Boxers.

Landing parties of some 900 marines were readied, and nine

small gunboats were deployed upriver, above the forts. The American naval elements on the scene had been forbidden by their government to participate. The Chinese commandant of the forts opened fire first, one hour after midnight and one hour before the expiration of the allied ultimatum. The forts fell, and four new, Chinese navy, German-built destroyers were captured by the invaders on June 17. This night action at Taku was an important naval victory, ensuring a line of communications that, in turn, allowed rescue of the Tientsin concessions, Admiral Seymour's force, and the Peking legations.

The reactions were felt elsewhere. Admiral Seymour's column endured increased enemy pressure on June 18. Von Ketteler was struck down in the street, and the Peking siege began on June 20. China declared war on the Allies on June 21.

The efforts of the Europeans in the Tientsin foreign concessions to defend themselves were vigorous and timely. Fortunately, a body of Russian troops, which had been sent on to follow Admiral Seymour, arrived too late to join Seymour, but just in time to prevent the capture of the railway station by the Boxers. Concurrent with the allied taking of the Taku Forts on June 17, the Tientsin foreigners were hit by heavy attacks by Chinese and Boxer forces that continued over several days. However, with Admiral Seymour's 2,100 men (largely British) in the Hsiku Arsenal and some 2,400 troops (largely Russian) in the Tientsin concessions and with the arrival ashore on June 23 of 8,000 more allied troops, the Chinese and Boxer pressure eased.

Tientsin's concessions were reinforced, Admiral Seymour's besieged troops were rescued, and operations were undertaken in late June to clear out the environs of Tientsin. By mid-July, an attack could be mounted on Tientsin's native city, which fell in bitter fighting by July 14. By mid-July, however, inaccurate reports and wild rumors in the press had convinced the outside world that all the foreigners in Peking had already been massacred.

The Allies did not immediately strike out for Peking. The battle for Tientsin had been hard. After Seymour's experience, the Allies knew that they needed strong reinforcements, supplies, and equipment, which were still arriving off Taku. Most of them were not due until August; further, the Americans and the other Europeans did not want the Russians and Japanese, with the majority of the troops already on the scene, to steal the glory before they themselves could participate honorably.

This was the setting, then, when Lieutenant Steel, General Gaselee, and the other participants in the allied relief expedition marched north out of Tientsin towards Peking on August 4, 1900. Steel's diary entries tell us of that action.

Peking Occupied

Lieutenant Steel has given us a personal account of the British entry into Peking, perhaps the key or most important one. The British troops were fortunate to get in at a lightly defended gate to the Chinese City, to march unimpeded westwards, and to arrive at their own legation compound through the Sewer Gate tunnel (Plate 11). The Russians, who tried to beat the gun on the other nations in the race to Peking and the glory of rescue, could not maintain a straight course to their assigned gate, confusing all. The Japanese, whose ten thousand men comprised half the total forces, and the Americans, who first had to scale the towering Chinese City wall, also broke in from the east. French troops, primarily diminutive, exhausted Tonkinese, straggled in, urged along by their officers. The major body of the Germans had not yet arrived in North China, and so only a token force was on hand, along with a few Austrians and Italians.

As the foreigners burst in, enemy opposition melted away from in front of the legations off to the north and apparently out the northern gates of Peking. The various military commanders established contact with their diplomatic counterparts and tried to decide what might be their next military and diplomatic objective. The Americans, under General Chaffee, battered their way into the Imperial City, but were halted before entering the innermost courtyards of the palace by a decision of the diplomats. Apparently remembering the shameful looting and burning of the Summer Palace in 1860 and recognizing that they must preserve some dignity, site, and symbol of continuing Chinese sovereignty, the ministers called off the soldiers.

Another military objective remained, the besieged Pei-t'ang, or northern, Roman Catholic cathedral, two miles to the northwest of the legations (Plate 34). Here Bishop Favier, 2 officers, 41 French and Italian sailors, about 100 Europeans, and originally some 3,300 Chinese converts had held their perimeter in a heroic defense, surpassing the achievement of the legations. They had never been allowed any respite from continuous, brutal, and horrifying attack, as had the legations, and their food stocks were pitifully meagre. The relief of the cathedral was casually delayed until August 16. Japanese troops inadvertently preceded the French, supported by Russians and Britishers, in relieving the Pei-t'ang.

Others have written of the siege of the legations, and this is not the burden of Lieutenant Steel's diary. However, it should be considered in outline. It lasted from June 20 until August 14, with a curious, unexplained truce occurring in the last two weeks of July. There were gallant heroes; unspeakable horrors and suffering born by the sick and wounded; self-sacrificial labors performed by amateur, volunteer civilians; wise administrative delegations of tasks to specialist committees; and ingenious solutions to problems of food, reinforcements, and communications. But there were shameful inequities, as well. Some did not do their share; there was insufficient food to allocate to the refugee Chinese Christian converts; there were episodes that were close to mutiny; national differences, eccentricities, and bickerings endangered the safety of all.

There were occasions when it seemed that a tiny, incremental effort by the enemy might have let all the murderous horde in for the kill at some vulnerable corner or salient. Perhaps the siege was not conducted in wholehearted fashion, and certainly it was done haphazardly and ineffectively. In the end, perhaps the empress dowager and Jung-lu, in a psychological or subconscious sense, refrained from backing the final push that would result in a massacre of the foreigners. They would have been haunted by the thought of the ferocity and the magnitude of the retribution to be expected.

We shall read in Lieutenant Steel's pages several references to acquisitions of art, artifacts, curios, china, silk, furs, and silver. He loyally acquired and sent off several boxes of treasures to Lord Curzon, not thinking of himself. But the aftermath of the relief of the siege has a distinct flavor of materialism, of shopping, of collecting *things*. It could only be expected that these occupation troops began now to think of themselves and their own welfare—all the while harboring tremendous indignation against the Boxers and other Chinese who had so barbarously and callously tried to wipe out the legations.

Great wealth abounded in Peking, and it would have taken saints to control the soldiery from looting One nation might try to discipline its own representatives with threats of courts-martial or directives to turn all acquisitions into a pool of prizes. Observing the conduct and violations of other soldiers of other nations, however, national inhibitions would break down. The possibilities were too tempting. In short, the post–August 14 story of Peking reads "looting." Lieutenant Steel only hinted at what went on among the rank and file. Certain high officials, as well, with better facilities at hand to ship home the loot, ensured their futures.

And then there was the task, possibly the sport, of chasing Boxers. The Germans, with their forces now built up under the supreme commander Field Marshal Count von Waldersee (Plate

20), justified their fervor over von Ketteler's murder. They responded to the personal exhortations of the kaiser himself and were resentful that they were late to get to Peking.

Major General Wilson, a new U.S. commander, and Waldersee personally led punitive expeditions to eliminate Boxer strongholds, chastise villages who had been hostile to missionaries and to Christian converts, and exact retribution. Inevitably, one suspects, many innocents suffered and most of the guilty evaded punishment.

The Empress Dowager's Flight and Peace Proposals

The empress dowager, Tz'u-hsi, and her court fled from Peking in the early morning of August 15. No plans had been made, and she clad herself in the simple clothes of a country woman and departed in a peasant's cart. She repeated the flight of forty years earlier, when she, as a young concubine, had accompanied a previous royal party in flight from the foreigners. This time, after a miserable and humiliating start, she began, month by month, to accumulate again the luxuries, the followers, and the perquisites of her position. The court in exile moved to the north, then west to Sian, Shensi, becoming a "tour of inspection." Meeting Yü-hsien, the Shansi governor and former supporter of Boxers, the empress dowager's comment is reported to have been that the price of coffins was going up, a euphemistic reference to the bitter fact that someone was going to have to answer to the allies, if not she herself. She continued to command obeisance, and the communications again poured in, as she governed the realm and received the peace proposals of the allies. She returned with great pomp to Peking in November 1901.

After the fighting, the allies selected their delegations for the peace talks, generally choosing the same individuals who had endured the siege. An exception was the choice of Sir Edward

Sato, formerly in Tokyo, to replace Sir Claude MacDonald as British minister.

The basic objectives of the powers were to ensure punishment of the offending Chinese and Boxer leaders, to secure an indemnity for the expenses of the allied relief expedition, and to revise the existing treaties. By Christmas 1900, some twelve points had been agreed upon by the Allies: China was to send a mission to Berlin to apologize for von Ketteler's murder, a similar apology was to be made to Japan for Sugiyama's murder, punishment was to be meted out to the Boxers and their supporters, no examinations were to be allowed for five years in former Boxer areas, expiatory monuments were to be erected for the dead foreigners, China could not bring in arms, an indemnity would be assessed, a new legation quarter was specified, certain communications strongpoints would continue under allied occupation, measures would be taken to curb antiforeignism, there would be new commercial trade arrangements, and the Tsungli Yamen would be reorganized (Plate 37).

On the Chinese side, Prince Ch'ing and Li Hung-chang (Plate 17) were the primary negotiators. The allies' conditions were met bit by bit, through the mechanism of several decrees, in order to save face for the Manchu regime. The final peace protocol was signed on September 7, 1901.

Occupation Duty

Lieutenant Steel spent the winter of 1900–1901 in Peking. The chapter of his diary over that time can be considered as a tourist's or traveller's view of that most renowned of Chinese cities.

There is authentic record of settlement on the site of Peking as early as the twelfth century B.C. It was a logical site for a city capital of a buffer state to keep the Tartar hordes out of the agricultural lowlands adjacent to the coast on the Bay of Chihli. In the thirteenth century, Kublai Khan built the city anew as the capital of his Mongol Empire. The Peking of Lieutenant Steel's time, however, was rebuilt by Yung-Lo, the second Ming emperor, in the early fifteenth century. Matteo Ricci, the first Jesuit father to get into China, arrived in Peking in January 1601. The Manchus, after their conquest of the Mings in 1644, transferred their rule from Mukden to Peking. Peking was the target of the foreigners invading China in 1860 in order to secure recognition by the emperor, as well as during the time of the present diary.

Peking was easy to comprehend, because of its uniform orientation, spacious symmetry, and rectangular ground-plan, as may be seen from the map between pp. 54 and 54. The northern section, or Tartar City, was a square, protected by towering walls about four miles on a side. The southern section, or Chinese City, was an oblong, east and west, with walls fourteen miles in length, including the four miles of the south wall of the Tartar City. The Imperial City was another square with six and one-half miles of walls within the Tartar City, and within the Imperial City lay the Forbidden City, with its many imperial palaces.

A moat outside the western walls was fed itself by a canal from the Western Hills and led water into seven lakes, north to south, inside the Tartar City. We shall read of Lieutenant Steel ice-skating on the lakes and riding his horse or pony in and out of the many city gates, or *men,* as they are termed in Chinese. He rode in and out of the Legation Quarter, adjacent to the south wall of the Tartar City; south to the Temple of Heaven and the Altar (or Temple) of Agriculture, where British and American troops were encamped in the southern Chinese City; and to other interesting points, such as the Lama Temple, the Drum Tower, and Coal Hill (Plates 33, 35, and 36).

One is inevitably very sensitive to or conscious of geography in Peking. The Great Wall of China, an ancient physical barrier and still perhaps a symbolic or psychological barrier, between

Han China and the Tartar hordes of Mongolia and Manchuria, lay in the mountainous foothills only thirty-five miles to the north of the city. The lakes of Peking flowed off into canals and the drainage system of the Pei Ho, which allowed junk transport and access to Tientsin and the Bay of Chihli. The airborne dust of the winter and spring atmosphere reminded one that the western deserts were close. Lieutenant Steel, wrote of the completion of the rail network, linking Peking to the southwest to Paotingfu and to the southeast to Tientsin. Within the city itself, the streets ran north and south and east and west. After Steel's time, but before the modern era, one told a ricksha puller to "go north" or "go west" but never "turn left" or "at the next block go right." All knew their geography.

We shall also read of the Summer Palace. This is not the *old* Summer Palace, the Yüan-ming-yüan, laid out with Western-style buildings in imitation of Versailles by the Italian Jesuit artist and architect, Castiglione. After it had been looted and pillaged by invading troops and villagers in 1860, Lord Elgin's Anglo-French forces had burned its 200 buildings. Lieutenant Steel visited the *new* Summer Palace, the I-ho-yüan, built as a retreat for the empress dowager in 1889. Funds, supposedly for the Chinese navy, had been diverted into the Summer Palace project (Plate 39). In 1900, we find it garrisoned by British and Italian troops, no destruction having been done to it. It was a favorite countryside resting place for General Gaselee and his staff.

Lieutenant Steel continued as an aide or orderly officer. Garrison life again resembled his life in India, with many social occasions, gallant treatment of the ladies, and resumption of sports and games—this time with a decided international flavor.

In the background, other events were transpiring. The looting of Peking had probably now diminished into mere souvenir hunting, but other punitive actions were underway. Expeditions went out into the countryside to mete out punishment to Boxers and their supporters. Leaders were stripped of their honors, banished into exile, ordered to commit suicide, executed, or posthumously dishonored. But the empress dowager herself was allowed to return to the imperial capital.

Differences sprang up between the allies, centering generally over whether China was to be treated as a free trade area for all or whether the old monopoly areas and spheres of influence were to be continued. Lieutenant Steel hinted of these issues when he wrote of Russian and French troubles in Tientsin. The Germans, under Field Marshal Count von Waldersee, were intent on proving themselves severe in their occupation policies, but the good count undoubtedly mellowed when he finally found company and personal contentment with a lovely young courtesan. Russia strove to establish Manchuria as a "closed door," a Russian zone. This policy pushed Japan into the position of Far Eastern ally of Britain, and it was to lead to the clash between Russia and Japan of 1904.

Britain, through the inspiration of Alfred Hippisley, who worked with his friend the new U.S. minister, William W. Rockhill, was instrumental in persuading U.S. Secretary of State John Hay to a new "Open Door" policy for China. Superficially it appeared as a "hands-off" attitude, but in actuality China was soon opened even more to trade and railroad building. The Boxers were gradually forgotten. The United States applied the Boxer indemnity sums to scholarships for Chinese students.

Departure

Years in India and months in China wore down the state of Lieutenant Steel's health. He was uncomplaining, but apparently felt debilitated and fatigued and was perhaps suffering from jaundice. We read, too, of the necessity for him to consult dentists.

The last chapter of his adventure in China begins with his initial mention of a serious consultation with his doctor. Steel enjoyed another visit to the Summer Palace and made his preparations for leaving Peking. There were many friends to whom to say farewell. The charm of Peking in the spring was most certainly marred by the fine, wind-blown dust from the western deserts, which permeated everywhere.

On this last trip south, he was able to travel on the restored railway line (Plates 14 and 15) to Tientsin and the Taku forts. A coastal steamer took him to Chefoo and to Shanghai, where there were more goodbyes to be said. He departed China on April 28, 1901, on board the *Empress of India*.

Lieutenant Steel returned to England, making short stops in Japan and crossing Canada by rail and steamer on the lakes. He took time out to indulge in his enthusiasm for fishing and met many western frontier personalities new to him. More importantly, however, he met a young lady from New Zealand, Adine Acton-Adams, travelling to England with her mother. She later was to become his wife.

His return to his home and to his family members was joyous. He enjoyed and profited from his year of medical leave, regaining his health. A part of that time was spent in Germany, near Freiburg, on language study.

Later in his military career he attended the staff course at Camberley, England, was a language student in Japan, served on regimental duty in India, was on the staff of the crown prince of Germany on the latter's Indian tour, received the award of the Red Eagle of Prussia, and was invited to East Prussia in 1912 to enjoy another of his passions, shooting. He was military attaché in Teheran in 1913–14, saw active service in France on the staff of the Indian Division, was on the staff of the Thirty-fifth Division, "Kitchener's Army," in the United Kingdom, and was at the War Office, London. He retired as colonel in 1920 and died in 1928.

Through Peking's Sewer Gate

1

Arrival In China, July 15–26, 1900

15 July 1900 Sunday Arrived at Hong Kong about 4 p.m. and anchored in the harbour abreast of H.M.S. *Bonaventure*. I landed with Creagh, 4th Punjab Infantry, formerly in the Hong Kong Reg't., and went to the Club, which is a very fine building. Then crossed to Kowloon and dined with the Hong Kong Reg't.

16 Monday Went on shore early with General Gaselee, General Barrow [Plate 24], and Pell to an informal inspection of the Hong Kong Reg't., a very fine looking lot, very big men and splendidly housed in first-class, stone-built barracks. Kowloon, where they are, is on the mainland, one mile from Hong Kong, and a ferry steamer crosses every ten minutes. I went across to Hong Kong after breakfast with the H.K. Reg't. and did a few purchases. Hong Kong, or rather Victoria, is a splendid looking city after Calcutta, so solid and clean looking. There is a total absence of horses, rickshaws drawn by Chinamen taking their place—Sikh policemen. I dined at the Club with Rigby and Stodhart and slept on board. We made a fruitless attempt to get the horses off after lunch, but the arrangements were impossible.

17 Tuesday I went on shore with the General and General Barrow, but came off almost directly to the ship. I did some more shopping and returned on board. I went ashore with Phillipps and brought back the order for the ship to get out into the harbour, as she was in Kowloon docks. [They were in a hurry, or should have been in a hurry. The siege of the Peking legations had begun on June 20.] I again went on shore with Low, and we went to the Club and then up by the rope tramway to the Peak, which is the highest point in Hong Kong, some 2000-odd feet above sea level. We were invited to lunch at the Peak Hotel by Colonel O'Gorman and afterwards went up in "chairs" to the flag staff. A most splendid view of all the islands, etc., and ripping air. Went with Pell after tea to call on H.M.S. *Dido* and saw some very good charts of the Pei Ho.

18 Wednesday I went to the *Dido* and borrowed four large-scale charts from Creagh-Osborne, the navigating lieutenant, and spent all morning tracing them with Norie, the Deputy Assistant Quartermaster General for Intelligence. I took them off again on completion and then went ashore and paid my bill at the Club.

Sir Alfred came on board for lunch, and we sailed at 3, the ships in harbour and we saluting one another. The Lymoon pass, through which vessels pass to eastward, is very narrow and strongly fortified—a Brennan torpedo shoot [land-emplaced torpedo tubes] and many mines and searchlights, etc. Very pretty scenery as we passed out—the water studded with junks.

20 Friday We were stopped off the mouth of the Yangtze Kiang [River] by H.M.S. *Bonaventure,* 2nd Class Cruiser, at 3. a.m. (Saturday), who was lying out to intercept us. She brought news from Shanghai that decided Sir Alfred Gaselee to go there. He, General Barrow, and Captain Pell A.D.C. [aide-de-camp] accordingly went on *Bonaventure,* we going on towards Weihaiwei at 5 a.m.

21 Saturday En route Weihaiwei. I got up the entire mess kit and the kit of Generals Gaselee and Barrow and got them ready to land.

22 Sunday Arrived at Weihaiwei at about 5 p.m. The harbour is formed by the island of Liukungtao, which lies across its mouth. The *Itinda,* with 12th Field Battery Royal Artillery, was in harbour and H.M.S. *Terrible.* Colonel Prendergast, Royal Engineers, is commdg. officer and commissioner. *Itinda* started for Taku with battery.

23 Monday I landed on the island at 10 a.m. with Captain Norie. The island is about one and one-half miles long and hilly. The forts are practically in the same state that the Japanese left them in, after taking them from the Chinese. The pier and landing accommodations are very bad, vessels of over fifteen feet draught not being able to get alongside. At the end of the pier are the remains of a Chinese man-of-war sunk by the Japanese, which our sailors are trying to blow up and get rid of. The houses are good, built of granite and altogether much cleaner and better than I expected—a few Chinese and Japanese shops. The hospital is good and filled with wounded from Tientsin, chiefly naval brigade, Marines and Royal Welch Fusiliers. I landed in the evening, borrowed a bike from a ship's officer, and had a spin.

24 Tuesday Early H.M.S. *Bonaventure* came in with Sir Alfred on board. H.M.S. *Centurion,* flagship, arrived shortly after. I went on board with Sir. A., who consulted for a long time with Admiral Seymour. [Vice Adm. Sir Edward Hobart Seymour had led the first, unsuccessful relief column out of Tientsin.] I had a very graphic account of the taking of Hsiku Arsenal, etc., during the retirement of Admiral Seymour's (relieving) force on Tientsin, from Major Johnstone, Royal Marine Light Infantry, in *Centurion*. He and all others eulogized Japanese bravery and splendid medical and other arrangements. The Russians, they said, were very slow and had done a good deal of wanton damage and slaughter. We heard today of the taking of Tientsin City and of very heavy losses sustained by the Powers. And great slaughter of Chinese. We landed the General and inspected sites for a

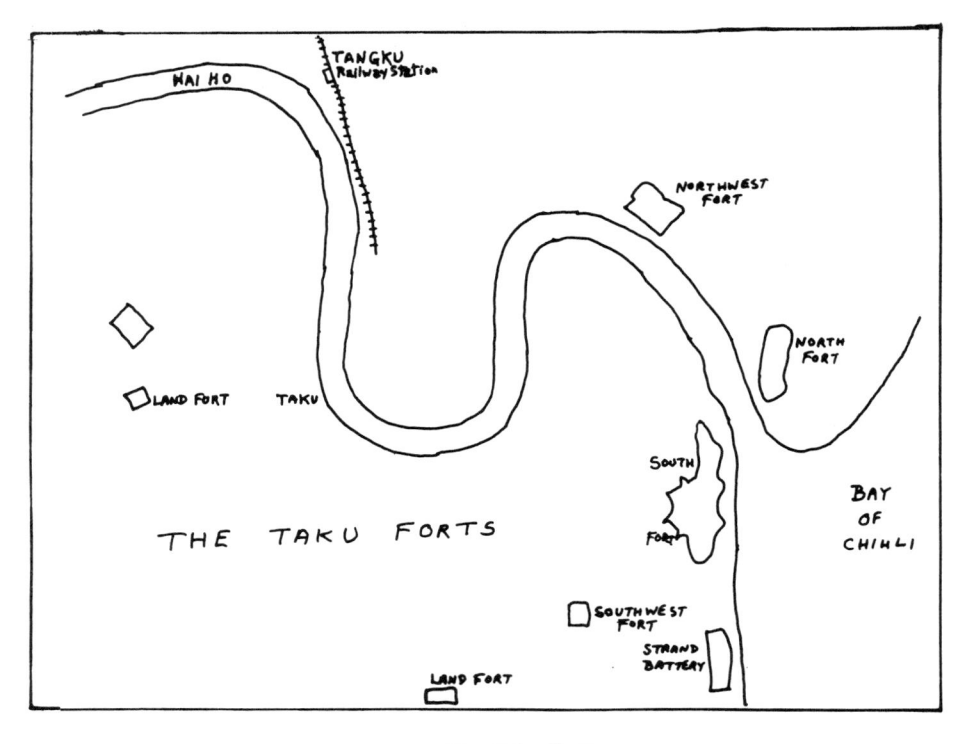

The Taku Forts

hospital. I lunched with Colonel Prendergast. We started for Taku at 6 p.m., *Centurion* going to Shanghai.

25 Wednesday We arrived off Taku (twelve miles) and anchored by H.M.S. *Barfleur* and one other ship in the middle of the Allied Fleets at 4 p.m. The Russians, French, German, Japanese, Italians, Austrians, Americans, and ourselves are represented—a most magnificent sight. The Chinese man-of-war, breech bolts of guns removed and engine disabled, was lying with them. The General went off to Admiral Bruce in *Barfleur*. We are ready to disembark tomorrow.

26 Thursday Began 6 a.m. getting kit off and on board a small steamer which can cross bar and go up the river. Got all horses, mules, and baggage on board at 12 noon. I went in charge of horses and General's and Headquarters Staff kit. We steamed in and passed the Taku Forts, which are very formidable and don't look much battered about. The flags of all nations are flying on them. The Pei Ho is *very* muddy and much smaller than I expected. We passed many war vessels of all nations. The river takes many twists, and the banks are mere swampy salt marshes. The Russian flag is flying over the town of Taku, which was nearly deserted. We got up to Sinho, where our little base and landing stage is, and disembarked kit and horses. I got the horses groomed and well hand-rubbed for the first time. I dined on board the little steamer and slept there.

2

The Move from the Taku Forts to Tientsin, July 27–August 3, 1900

27 July Friday Reveille, 4:30 a.m. Got all horses and baggage on trucks at 7:30 a.m. Got to Tangku station at 8 a.m. The line from Taku to Tientsin is entirely managed by Russians. Russian troops are all along line to Tientsin. Some American officers of the 12th Reg't. were in the same carriage with us. [U.S. units variously present were the First Marines, Ninth Infantry, and parts of the Fourteenth Infantry, Sixth Cavalry, and Fifth Artillery.] We got to Tientsin station about 12 noon. Station was absolutely wrecked by shell during the bombardment. All villages along line were burnt and pillaged. We got off our baggage and horses, and I got the house in which General Gaselee and staff are staying and stacked kit and put up horses in a yard, with guard of sowars [Indian cavalrymen]. Every house has two or three shells thro' it. And the Pei Ho is full of dead Chinese, smelling horribly. I drove the General to confer with the Japanese generals 4 p.m. Saw horses groomed. Called on the British consul for General. Heard that the Legations in Peking were still safe on 21st, a letter having come thro' from MacDonald. The General held consultation with American, Jap, and French generals. Dined with General Dorward. [Brig. A.F.R. Dorward had led forces two weeks earlier in taking Tientsin.] Met Bower and Layard of the Chinese Reg't. [known also as the Weihaiwei Regiment, with British officers and Chinese troops]. A general movement to relieve Legations is nearly settled.

28 Saturday Got up very early and got the Headquarters horses, etc., into order. The General and General Barrow were very busy all morning conferring with the American general. Colonel Vogack, Russian, who has been in Tientsin for twelve years, came to lunch and went with the General and General Barrow and self to the Gordon Hall, whence all signalling was done in siege. Gordon Hall was full of wounded from the city fight, all doing fairly well. Colonel Vogack pointed out all points of interest, Russian and other camps, etc. The General went out, Pell and I going with him on horseback, to see the 7th Rajputs and 1st Sikhs, who are in the "concession." The American 12th and 9th Reg'ts. officers brought round their band after dinner, and we gave them drinks and had a very amusing talk, the band ending up with "God Save the Queen" and the Yankee National Anthem. Saw 12th Field Battery Royal Artillery.

29 Sunday Took out my horses for exercise and paraded all horses and their kits. Went to leave General's cards on the commanding officer and 9th Reg't. officers. Rode round in evening with Generals Gaselee and Barrow to the railway station and visited the scene of the fights. The engine shed was absolutely riddled with shell. Rode thro' the French concession, and back past American lines. Saw 12th Battery fellows.

[*On this date, July 29, Lieutenant Steel also found time to write to his brother, as follows. Although he reports on some items already covered in the diary entries, the letter is a good review of what he has just seen and done.*]

Tientsin July 29, 1900

My dear old Brother,

As I can only find time to write one long letter at odd intervals, I am writing to you this time and hope you will send it on to Grannie and Uncle Hal. I can hardly realize yet what an extraordinary jump I've made from the peaceful life in Simla into these stirring times.

We arrived on the 25th from Weihaiwei and anchored twelve miles out at sea off the mouth of the Pei Ho, where the Taku Forts are, in the middle of the Allied Fleets—English, Russian, German, French, Japanese, Austrian, and Italian. Large vessels cannot go further, so next morning we transferred our horses, mules, and baggage on to a light steamer and started at 12 o'clock.

The Fleet is a most magnificent sight, and we saw the four destroyers captured by us and presented to the Germans, Russians, and French. The Taku Forts show signs of hammering, as you may suppose, but the big guns are still on the walls and the flags of the various Powers fly on different parts. The Pei Ho is an insignificant, muddy stream. There are *very* flat mud flats on either side, covered with salt heaps. We passed a lighter which the Russians had sunk and drowned five hundred coolies.

The river winds about a great deal, and the country is dead flat. The town of Taku is on the left going up, just behind the fort on the left of my sketch, and Tangku, which is the location of the railway to Tientsin, is a little higher upstream. The Russians hold Taku and Tangku and are working the railway up to Tientsin, having been wily enough to have a railway battalion handy and send it on at once.

Our landing place and depot is at Sinho, on the left bank of the river (right as you are going up), and there lies H.M.S. *Algerine* that did all the good work going at the Taku Forts. We disembarked that night and had a very comfortable time, my hands being full of the Headquarters Staff horses and baggage. The General, General Barrow, and Pell, the other ADC, went up by river at once in the launch belonging to the *Algerine* after dining on board. All the other staff officers and I got on the rough train on a still rougher line rigged up in a hurry to Sinho, I having a real busy time with my horses and kit at 4:30 in the morning.

We were all in open coal trucks, and as it started to pour down rain, were somewhat uncomfortable, my guard of six men and I sitting on top of our baggage. Luckily I had a waterproof sheet and some biscuits and distilled water off the ship in my big water bottle, so was well off. We got in to the main line at 8, when we, the officers, transshipped into a second class carriage and were rather hospitably met by the Russian officers at the junction. The line just swarms with Russians, who compare very unfavourably with Britishers as to uniform and smartness, as indeed do all the different nations' soldiers here.

We got to Tientsin station about 12 and got out kit up to the different quarters in the town. The station is an *extraordinary* sight. The fighting there was fearful during the siege. The engine shed is like a sieve with shells, and the whole station burnt, sacked, and in ruins. We crossed the Pei Ho by a rough bridge, guarded by slovenly French soldiers, who told me they had just hauled out six Chinese bodies. The whole river is polluted with dead Chinese and all sorts of horrors. The town is practically in ruins, as far as the French quarter goes, and there are dozen of holes made by shell in each house in the British concession. Everything is fearfully unsanitary and in ruins in Tientsin, and the city which I haven't seen was, of course, gutted and looted after the taking.

The Japanese have about nine thousand men; the Russians, about six thousand, I believe. We and the Americans, fifty-five hundred; and the Germans, three hundred, etc. The French they say, don't count, as the Americans put it, "I guess they get *cold feet* when the guns pop!" The Japs are splendid little chaps. Their arrangements are wonderful, and they are as keen as can be. Of course it is fearfully difficult to get concerted action between all the Powers. The Japs, Americans, and we ourselves are in perfect accord, and I think the Russians mean to play up.

We heard that the Legations were safe on the 22nd, a runner having got thro', but they had very many killed and wounded and could not last out more than a fortnight. Of course we are most anxious to start at once, or as soon as we can, but with so few men it is rather hazardous, I think. The country will be most difficult if we have any more rain. Water is bad, and there are at least sixty thousand Chinese between this and Peking. It is a great mistake to suppose the Chinese are contemptible. They have hundreds of the most modern guns, big and otherwise, even Maxims with galloping carriages, thousands of Mauser rifles, and ammunition without count.

The General and Pell, the other ADC, went out this morning

with a reconnaissance in force by the Japanese and have just come in. They went out about seven miles, and the Japanese brigade attacked a Chinese position, losing three killed and about ten wounded only. They say they can't see the Chinese a bit—they are so good at taking cover. We are to start the day after tomorrow, early, and take all baggage in junks up the river.

We are very limited as to kit. I have only a roll of bedding with a spare shirt or two, etc., and a waterproof sheet which I can rig up as a shelter. I wish you could see the place—soldiers of every nationality swarm everywhere, and the place is strewn with all sorts of property, cartridges, and loot of all kinds. The Americans are most friendly and jolly, and we had a visit from thirty of their officers the other night. They brought their band, and we all stood solemnly at attention for about fifteen minutes whilst they played "God Save the Queen" and the American tune (I forget it).

Goodbye, dear old chap. My very best love to dear Grannie and Uncle Hal and all at home.

Always,
Your loving brother, Dick

P.S. After all, Mother had better not see this. I'll send her another note.

30 Monday General Gaselee and several other officers went out with the reconnaissance in force of the Japanese [Plate 1] towards Peitsang, seven miles northwest of the city, starting 3 a.m. The Japs lost three killed and thirty wounded and came back about 2 p.m. I was busy packing all spare kit and taking it to the "godown" where it is to be stored. Found many .303 Mauser and other cartridges lying about there, several of the .303 being expensive ones. Lieutenant Keyes, Royal Navy, who commanded H.M.S. *Fame* (destroyer) at the taking of the Taku Forts and who took the four Chinese destroyers, came to be naval A.D.C. to Sir Alfred [Plate 18]. Walked over with Keyes in evening to the American 9th Infantry Headquarters. [Keyes was to become Admiral of the Fleet Lord Keyes, famed for the raid on Zeebrugge in 1918 and a naval advisor in World War II.]

31 Tuesday Went over with Keyes to the 9th Americans and got a certain amount of clothing for the servants. Got the General's guard on the boats we are allotted. I went out with General Barrow in evening, riding to call on the German Marine officers, and we were very hospitably entertained and spent some time talking bad German. The Japanese were out again, concluding their reconnaissance of yesterday, but we did not hear of any more casualties. General Barrow went to see Fukushima, the Jap general, and his chief of staff. The delay in advance is due to Russians, who retard all business. Strength here: Japs, eight thousand; English and Americans, about six thousand; Russians about six thousand? [It is elsewhere recorded that the allied relief force marched out of Tientsin on August 4 comprising roughly 10,000 Japanese; 4,000 Russians; 3,000 British; 2,000 Americans; 800 French; 100 Germans; and 100 Austrians and Italians.]

1 August Wednesday Got all followers clothing in morning and took Brinks [his horse] out for exercise along the Taku road, where there is any amount of green fodder (millet). The Japs and French and our drabies [corruption of "driver," Indian army] cut it. Went out in evening with General Barrow and Major St. John, Royal Artillery, as far as the Hsiku Arsenal, where Admiral Seymour was shut up four days during his retirement. Saw some signs of the Chinese in the distance. Rode back thro' the city, which is in ruins and any amount of foreign guards of all nationalities about it. St. John explained how the city was taken—a very fine performance—the gate which was blown in by the Japs, etc. Went round to see the Germans after dinner.

2 Thursday Worked all morning getting kit and boats, etc., ready and getting Union Jacks made (painted with Aspinall). Took all horses out to exercise and saw 12th Field Battery Royal Artillery drilling and Japanese.

I rode in the evening with Sir Alfred and General Barrow

and Bower to the city and round the quarter we are holding. Most *unutterable* filth and desolation everywhere. The suburbs are the worst part. Very high old walls round the city have been breached in places by our shells. Went round with about fifteen of our officers to visit the Americans after dinner and had a very cheery concert. We finished up with "Auld Lang Syne" and "God Save the Queen," very good business.

3 Friday Looked all morning at boats, etc., and rode out with Keyes along Taku road. I rode with Keyes out to Sinku, seven miles beyond this. The Naval Brigade with four twelve-pounders, Marines, and 24th Punjab Infantry bivouac there tonight [Plate 3]. We heard that it has been decided at a meeting of the Generals of the various Powers to advance tomorrow. We are to bivouac at Sinku tomorrow night. The 6th American Cavalry [only a portion arrived in time] arrived today and their battery. I met Cheyne and Gaussen of 1st Bengal Lancers.

3

The Military Attack from Tientsin to Peking, August 4–14, 1900

4 August Saturday Marched out of Tientsin with our whole force at 2:30 p.m. seven miles to Sinku and bivouacked there. It rained a good bit, and we were all pretty wretched in consequence. The English, Japanese, and Americans were on right bank of river; French and Russians on left. The General and all of us put up in a yamen [Chinese court or residence] for the night.

5 Sunday We got up at 1 a.m., pitch dark, and got out after some difficulty on a bund running to our left front. I was detailed as English representative, Orderly Officer, with Americans. Firing began at 3 a.m. on left front, the Japs being heavily engaged. Our batteries opened fire about 5 a.m. and were replied to by many guns from villages on the river. The Japs, who were on ahead, worked round to the enemy's right flank and carried first their powder arsenal [the Hsiku Arsenal, again] on the bund and then their main position splendidly. [See the accompanying copy of a field message on the assault, from Colonel Churchill to General Gaselee, and relayed by Lieutenant Steel to General Chaffee.] The firing was tremendous till about 9 a.m. The Chinese shell dropped all round us, one exploding within forty yards of General Chaffee, USA, with whom I was, killing one

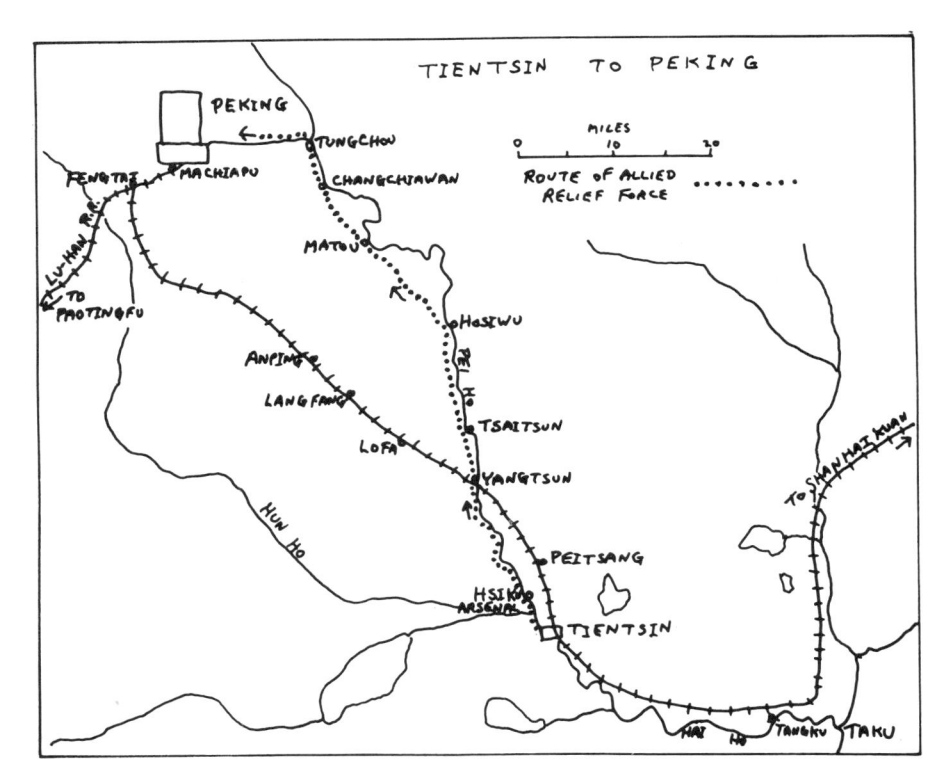

Tientsin to Peking

Jap and two horses and wounding many. [Maj. Gen. Adna R. Chaffee, a U.S. western frontier and Civil War veteran, was the commander of U.S. forces in China. He later became Chief of Staff of the U.S. Army.] The 12th Field Battery Royal Artillery came into action twice or three times, and the 24th Punjab Infantry and 1st Sikhs, supporting the Japs, drove the enemy from Peitsang, and we halted at a village about a mile north of Peitsang. The naval guns fired along the Peking road, at about six thousand yards, with some effect. We crossed a bridge of boats at Peitsang

發	月	日	午	時	分	發簡地	於
著	月	日	午	時	分		
著簡受	Genl. Gaselee Commg British Force					希簡發	5. a.m. Left flank

The *Arsenal after stubborn defence has just been carried with bayonet — The way is now open for a turn to the North of the Japanese troops — Suggest cavalry moving to this (~~left~~ our left) flank

　　　　　AJ Churchill Lyol

※ Powder Magazine

Field Message, 4 August 1900

and bivouacked there. The Japs lost about a hundred and fifty and we twenty-five.

6 Monday Next morning, Monday, we started at 6 a.m., along left bank of the Pei Ho. The Russian and French were in one column on left; the British in middle; Americans, left. I was with the Americans again. The Americans went down the railway track, which is absolutely wrecked, and we reached to within four miles of Yangtsun. The Americans then crossed the rail to right and swung round to right to meet a flanking fire from three or four villages, who opened a fairly hot fire with guns and rifles. The Americans then drove out the enemy with their guns, the 1st Bengal Lancers covering their right flank. The British made a frontal attack on the main position, carrying it grandly, the 1st Sikhs and 24th Punjab Infantry dashing at it splendidly. The American battery and a Jap battalion shelled the enemy retiring along the left bank, and we occupied Yangtsun, bivouacking on left bank. The Chinese carry away most of their dead and wounded, so we couldn't tell what damages we had done. It was the first day I had been under a fairly heavy fire and I confess I didn't feel comfortable for some time! Our losses were fifty killed and wounded (Costello, 1st Sikhs, badly). Americans, a little more. The Americans lost thro' not advancing quick enough, the dangerous zone being from eight hundred to fifteen hundred yards, where there was a perfect hail of bullets. The enemy cleared away wonderfully, leaving no guns.

8 Wednesday The Japanese started first from Yangtsun at about 5 a.m., followed by the Americans and then the British. I went with our force today. The road lay through Yangtsun and across a bridge of boats. The road was good, winding through fields of a very high millet, very difficult to get a view through. There was no opposition, and we camped on the river bank close to Tsaitsun. The Japanese occupied the village. A cipher message came in from Peking, to which there was no key. An officer of the 1st Bengal Lancers went in to Tientsin to get it deciphered by the vice consul. The Japanese got a message, too, saying the Legations were safe and had increased their ammunition to thirty rounds per man. Yangtsun was absolutely filthy, like every Chinese town, but filled with corpses of Chinese. The French remained behind in Yangtsun. The water transport junks came up in fine style.

9 Thursday We started at 7:30 a.m. The day was fearfully hot and the road was awful, sand and very high crops. The Japs went on ahead, and the Russians. The Chinese made a very short stand at Hosiwu. The 1st Bengal Lancers got well into them retiring, killing, it is reported, from fifty to one hundred in the crops and capturing four standards. After a fearfully trying march we bivouacked on the river. The Americans lost a lot of men dead and many sick from sunstroke and we lost a few. The road was along a highish bund, and towards the end we were a very mixed, straggling lot of all nationalities. The village by which we were camped had been partially prepared for defence, spades lying about, and when I got thro' I found a teapot full of hot tea(!), showing how little before they had left it. The junks came up at night.

10 Friday Hosiwu. We could not go on, as the men and transport and animals were absolutely exhausted, and the heat was fearful, worse than anything I have experienced in India. We stayed the whole day in camp, no shade, under shelters made of mats got from the village. The Russians and Japanese and our field battery and cavalry went on in morning. Arrangements were made by our sappers for blowing up an immense quantity of powder stored in a joss house in Hosiwu. The Americans marched about 2 p.m., and we marched at 6 p.m. Boyce Kup, the interpreter, took us across country along the Peking main road, a mere track thro' millet crops at least fourteen feet high. We had a very trying march, luckily full moon, and did not arrive in camp (fifteen miles) till 3 a.m., everything confusion, and lay down at once in the wet crops and slept. Heard the Battery lost seven horses, died in the traces during the day, and many cases of heat apoplexy and sunstroke. We were three miles away when the powder exploded, *tremendous*.

11 Saturday Spent the whole day in bivouac by the river at Matou. It rained a little and was cloudy, but the heat was very steamy and trying. Heard a great cannonade to the north at 1 and again at 3 p.m., and saw smoke of many villages burning from the field observatory. Marched at 5:30 p.m. and arrived at Changchiawan about 1 a.m. The Americans were already in camp. The Japanese had shelled the enemy out of Changchiawan and had gone on and shelled Tungchou without reply. The force bivouacked in a very swampy, damp bit of ground, very misty. The Headquarters, however, being in a slightly better place.

12 Sunday The Battery came in early and 1st Bengal Lancers from last camp, and we advanced together to Tungchou, on the banks of a backwater of the Pei Ho. The Chinese had mostly bolted from the city. We occupied houses in the suburbs, along the bank of the backwater and established a post and left men to garrison it and collect provisions and stores. The Headquarters Staff occupied a big house belonging to a merchant. There was a godown full of valuables of all description, but no one was allowed to take anything, all being put into the guard. Tungchou city itself was occupied by the Japanese, a large city with a high wall. The junks will, we hope, be up tomorrow. The combined generals had a conference today and decided on a reconnaissance in force tomorrow.

13 Monday Two guns of the 12th Field Battery Royal Artillery, 7th Rajputs, and three squadrons 1st Bengal Lancers went out early to join in the combined reconnaissance on the road to Peking. They are to stay halfway to Peking tonight, and the scheme is for the remainder of the Allied Forces to march out and bivouac with them tomorrow. We spent the day establishing the post. Orders are to march at 3:30 a.m. tomorrow. It rained in torrents from 8–9 p.m.

14 Tuesday We heard guns from 1 a.m. continuously in the Peking direction. Started at 4 a.m., the English and Americans south of the canal and the Russians and Japanese north. We struggled on somehow or other thro' tracks in the very high crops, *all* view being obstructed. We reached the place where our advanced force bivouacked last night about 9 a.m. and halted a short time. We then pressed on, with an advance guard of two guns under Wilson, 7th Rajputs, and 1st Bengal Lancers and came on to the canal and the Americans.

After a short delay we got on to a wide road parallel to the canal and south, and came to within about two thousand yards of the gate of the Chinese City. Here there were a few Chinese who opened up a dropping fire, but were soon cleared out by the guns. The infantry advanced and rushed at the gate, and we all crowded in, everyone mixed up. We streamed along the central roadway inside, bullets whizzing everywhere, from our own men and Americans on the right of us, sniping Chinese.

We halted when opposite the gate behind which the Legations are, and after a bit the General and all of us on his staff and a few Sikhs and 7th Rajputs went down a road at right angles and were led by a guide to the banks of a moat which surrounds the Tartar City walls. Here we came under a dropping fire from the right flank, but could just see the portion of wall said to be held by the Legation. A report had spread that the Legations had fallen, and when we saw the Union Jack and other flags on the wall, we thought it was a Chinese ruse to draw us on.

Suddenly a signalling flag appeared and began, ''Come in quickly by the sluice gate [Plate 11].'' We raised a cheer and dashed along a street parallel to the canal until opposite a sort of cut under the city wall, the mouth of a huge sewer opening into the canal. We all dashed across the canal, bullets fizzing and spitting all round, a small shell exploding in front of my nose, no harm done.

The sewer is absolutely *filthy,* and barred by a huge grating. However, the friendly Chinese who have been sheltering in the Legations came down and smashed the bars, and we crowded thro' and ploughed our way through the filth under the archway [Plate 23]. We were met the other side by a crowd of all nations cheering and shouting and were led thro' to the British Legation by Sir Claude MacDonald.

The sight in the Legations beggars description. Any amount of women, children, and men crowded round us, shaking hands and cheering till they were hoarse. The Chinese all round having recognized we were in, opened a tremendous musketry fire, and one couldn't hear oneself speak. However, no one minded at all. The shots were high and only two men were hit. I had another real good squeak when looking after the General's horse, a bullet hit ground just under my foot.

Everyone plies us with drink and tea and bread, etc. They have killed nearly all their mules and ponies for food, and we shall have to do with pony meat for a day or two until our own comes up.

The guns battered down the Ch'ien Men, and a company of the 1st Sikhs and the Maxims came thro' and found a crowd of Boxers and soldiers inside. These they simply mowed down. Later we got in two guns of the 12th Field Battery Royal Artillery and opened fire on some barricades, whence the Chinese were firing, and soon silenced them. We slept in a pavilion in front of Sir Claude's house, crowded with refugees, etc., the men being in an open space in front. The remainder of the force are in the "Temple of Heaven," in the Chinese City.

[*On August 18, Lieutenant Steel composed the following*

letter to Col. Arthur C. Borton, his uncle, then in India. It amplifies the diary details.]

Peking Aug. 18th 1900

My dear Colonel:

Very sorry not to have written before, but have been having no time to do anything in that way. We got in here, as you will have seen, long ago on the 14th, and you can imagine how glad we were to do so and find the Legations holding out. We started from Tientsin on the afternoon of the 4th and bivouacked that night seven miles out. The Japanese were on our left, Americans right, the Russians and French on the other side of the river. Something like this: [Here Lieutenant Steel provided a sketch.]

It was a beastly night, raining every now and then, and we started at 2 a.m. to attack their main position in somewhat confusion. I was attached to the American general's staff that day and waited a long time before they had room to advance behind the raised embankment to our left front. The enemy's guns opened at about 3:30 a.m., before it was light, they having taken the range of the embankment. The Japanese batteries and our own, the 12th Field Battery Royal Artillery, replied directly it was light, and the Japs shoved on splendidly and turned their right flank. The 7th Bengal Lancers and 1st Sikhs and 24th Punjab Infantry made a frontal attack. The enemy's fire from their guns was most accurate, shell after shell just topping the embankment and bursting the other side. One burst just a few yards from me, killing and wounding several followers and mules and made me feel devilish uncomfortable for a bit. I'd never seen a man killed before!

We shoved on and followed between the Japs and British, but by the time we came up the main position had been taken and we merely had to march on to Peitsang. The enemy had a lot of guns, several big ones, but cleared every one out except the Japs lost 150 to 200. The Japs are perfectly splendid, like little terriers, as keen and plucky as can be. Their wounded never uttered a sound, and I saw lots carried past me with horrible wounds, some actually joking with the stretcher bearers. Their whole arrangements are so wonderful. If a Jap is hit, there's always a doctor on the spot, mounted well, with panniers with the very latest surgical jinns [magic cures].

It was a very long trying day and fearfully hot and our men, as well as all the other nations, were falling out all around.

The British force crossed the river at Peitsang and bivouacked in and near the town which had been evacuated in a hurry by all Chinese. The enemy had opened sluices and flooded all low ground on the right bank of the river so the 1st Bengal Lancers couldn't pursue. We started early next morning in 3 parallel columns over more open country.

The Russians and French were near the river; British, in the centre; and the Americans, with whom I was again, on the right near the railway. The railway was entirely destroyed. Sleepers all removed, and rails too, and the embankment even dug into. We encountered no opposition to within 4 miles of Yangtsun, when the cavalry reported the enemy holding a position to our left of the railway in front of the village. The Americans crossed the line and were pushing on, when owing to defective reconnoitering we were caught by a fire from guns and infantry on our right rear. The 1st Bengal Lancers seemed to me *useless* that day. They were on our right flank and ought to have given information much earlier. The American battery wheeled round to the right and shelled the 3 villages, but we had a very hot time till the infantry came up, shells bursting all round and an incessant hum of Mauser bullets, mostly high. I got shelter behind a bit of a bank and was jolly glad when I found it.

The Americans lost a good many and when at last we managed to silence the guns and pound them a bit, the Chinese scooted so quickly we couldn't pick them up again. A Jap battery came up and we pushed on with the American one and shelled masses of the Chinese retiring.

I *cannot* understand even now how the 1st Bengal Lancers didn't get into them retiring. They *are* a slow lot. I know one cavalry regiment that would have cut the beggars up well. The 1st don't seem to be able to *move*. Their reconnoitering seems very poor, and all their horses, or nearly all, have sore backs. Their transport animals are much overladen, and thro' some mistake (I suppose) they had their tents—and such a rag tag and bobtail that would impede the movement of any force.

Whilst all this was going on on the right of the railway, the 12th Field Battery Royal Artillery opened fire on the enemy's main position on the left of the railway, getting replied to by heavy guns firing smokeless powder, and some smaller ones with black powder to draw fire. The 24th Punjab Infantry and 1st Sikhs then advanced and rushed the position splendidly, losing some fifty or sixty, and stopped near the rail bridge over the river.

The Russians and French arrived too late with their attack on the enemy's right flank, as usual! The Japs were mostly on the other side of the river and had no fighting.

We stayed at Yangtsun on the 7th, pulling the troops together and sending the wounded down to Tientsin by river. All our transport except obligatory mules was by river on junks and necessarily came up very slowly, each boat having to be towed up by Chinese and Japanese coolies. And the river—dirty little ditch—winds about very much and is very shallow.

We then had some fearful hot days, marching with little or no opposition—8th to Tsaitsun, 9th to Hosiwoo. Here the Chinese had made big entrenchments, but cleared out of them after a few shots. The 1st Bengal Lancers got into a rabble of them retiring that day among the great tall millet crops, sticking a good many and capturing some standards. The heat was *awful,* the whole road being littered with men fallen out, Americans, Japs, and ours. The country is so dense with crops we couldn't see anywhere, and the flies and bad water made life pretty sickening. Everywhere one came across dead bodies of Chinese and mules and horses in various degrees of foul decomposition. I nearly catted dozens of times. We couldn't go on, as men and beasts were absolutely cooked. On the night of the 10th there was a full moon to enable us to march to Matou, a long straggling column thro' millet fields. We might have been cut up dozens of times by an enterprising enemy. However, we got in about 3 a.m. and just dropped asleep where we were in the wet crops by the river.

The battery and 1st Bengal Lancers had gone ahead that day with the Japs, and seven of the battery horses fell dead in the traces from the heat. The Japs went on ahead on the 11th, and we heard a deal of cannonading to the front, which turned out to be the Japs clearing Changchiawan and Tungchou.

We marched again that night to Changchiawan and Tungchou, thirteen miles from Peking. Here we established a base and post, as the river only comes up as far as Tungchou towards Peking, and our boats had not come up. On the 13th a reconnaissance in force went out towards Peking, seven miles, as in the sketch, next sheet.

The advanced party was to stay out and were to have been joined next day, the 14th, by the main forces, who would advance together on the 15th. However, on the morning of the 14th at 2 a.m. we heard a tremendous cannonade going on, which turned out to be the Japs and Russians attacking a very strong position on the right. We got out to our advanced party at about 9 a.m. and advanced at once. Beyond a few dropping shots, we encountered no opposition up to the very gates of the Chinese City.

All this time a very severe engagement was going on on the right across the canal, the Japs and Russians being heavily engaged. The Chinese didn't expect us to advance south of the canal (and no one else did either), but by sheer good luck we blundered on thro' dense country and mere tracks right up to the east gate of the Chinese City. The battery fired some dozen shots, and the Chinese scuttled, and we burst the door open and were inside.

There was a long, broad, straight road in front, along which we streamed east to west—no order, men and beasts absolutely done, 'till we reached a point where we halted and all sorts of reports spread—that the Legations had been scuppered, etc. The General then took a company of the 1st Sikhs and all of us on his staff, and we turned down a street to the right, bearing bang up to the wall of the Tartar City. The walls of the Tartar City are about seventy or eighty feet high and have a filthy moat all round.

Just as we neared the moat, the sniping which had been incessant, simply popped all round us, and we got shelter in a narrow lane, whence we could just see a glimpse of the part of the wall said to be held by the Legations. The American, French, Russian, and English flags were flying on the wall, but everyone said it was a Chinese ruse and that the legations had fallen. Suddenly a flag appeared above the wall and spelt out, "Come in quickly by the sluice gate into the moat."

We dashed along the narrow street parallel to the moat and suddenly saw a sewer opening thro' the wall into the moat. We all made a dash across the moat, the Chinese pouring in a hail of fire when they saw what we were up to. We got across also safe into the drain. It is a tunnel under the wall with the most *foul* slime and sewage, a couple of feet thick, barred by a grating. However, very willing hands inside pulled the grating to bits, and we were in the very first—hours ahead of any other nation.

There was a roaring, cheering crowd of every nationality inside, and we just cheered ourselves hoarse. We all got into the British Legation and were looked after and given drinks by the ladies inside.

Everyone was standing talking and cheering, a motley crowd, whilst the bullets were flying thick overhead and banging on the roofs all high, no one caring a hang! The Chinese simply went mad when they realized we were in and let off every bally gun they had at random.

I had a dozen near shaves, one bullet hitting the earth under my boot, but we only had two men hit. Meanwhile the whole of the rest of the force was in the Chinese City, only our handful inside. But they soon got the guns up, bashed in the big south gate and got well into a crowd of Chinese behind with 2 Maxims and a hundred Sikhs.

The sight inside next morning was ghastly, dead Chinese lying in all directions. The poor people in the Legations had had eight weeks incessant rifle fire and occasional bombardment. They had killed all except one racing pony for food, and the sanitary arrangements are something *awful*.

We spent all next day driving the Chinese out of various quarters, an immense job, as remember, each *face* of the Tartar City is four miles. And yesterday we took the Imperial City. Only the holy of holies, the Palace, remains untouched, by common agreement.

The loot is fabulous, but we are not allowed to touch anything. Regular foraging parties go out and bring in valuables, etc., but the Japs and French are before us, the brutes. I daresay I shall be able to buy some things cheap. I hope so. I have got a certain amount of curiosities. We got about £2000 worth of bar silver quite close here, which goes to the Prize Fund, but I hear the Japs and French have got a tremendous amount.

There is a rumour today that the Chinese are massing south of the Chinese City, and I am just going with Sir Alfred to see the dispositions. The Chinese will get an awful slating if they try any games now. I don't think they are such fools.

I have had a rather bad time for a couple of days with a bad boil on my ankle, but am all right again now and glad to be about. I think this will be a long, wearisome business. It will certainly mean sitting in Peking until a responsible government is established. I hope we shall get a few more troops from the line of communications. The Chinese might cut in there it seems any day.

I hope this will reach you all right. I have not stamps as we have not got a post office yet. Will you please send this on to Colonel Muir and his fellows in my reg't., as I can't write, and then to Sir

Robert Hume? I hope you will not think me bothering you. I hope you are comfortably settled down at Sralkote now. I jolly well wish I was back in India—all the show is over.

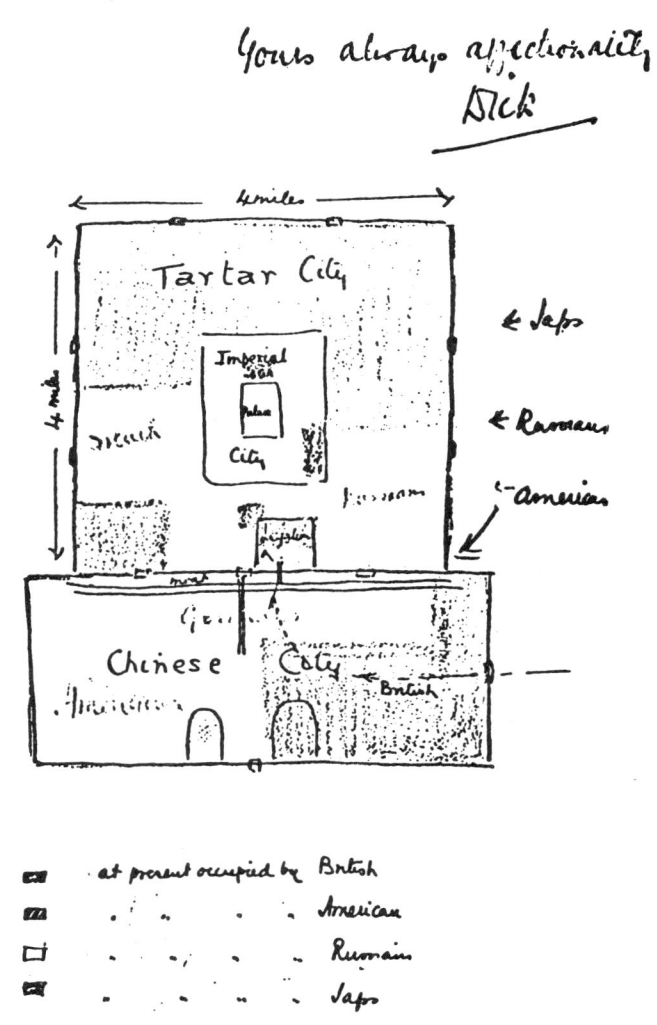

Yours always affectionately,
Dick

Last Page of Letter Lieutenant Steel Wrote to His Uncle, with Sketch of Peking

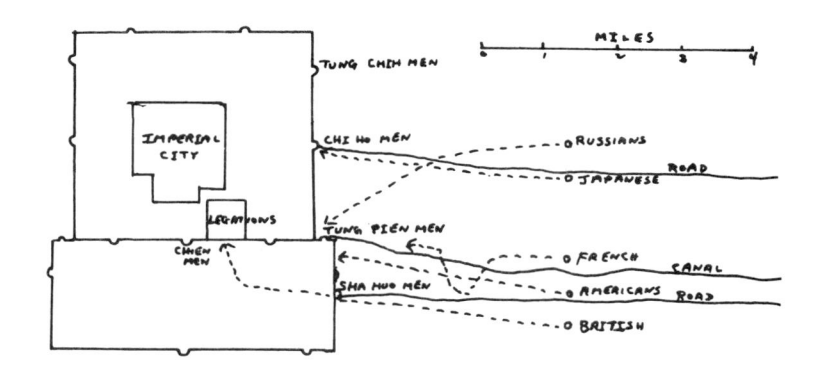

Allied Approach to Peking; the Legations

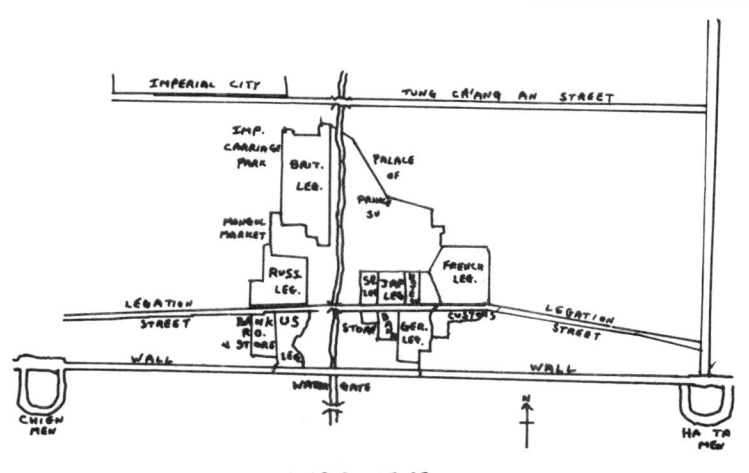

27

THE INTERNATIONAL FORCE

Plate 1. Japanese Infantry. They are posed with a Major Low, of the Ninth Bengal Lancers.

Plate 2. U.S. Troops. These Americans were on duty within the Forbidden City

Plate 3. Punjabi Infantry. They display a variety of uniforms.

Plate 4. Australian Contigent. They served as a naval unit.

Plate 5. Allied Troops. They apparently posed to show the international nature of the relief force. (Official photograph.)

Plate 6. Italian Officers. The Italians, shown with General Gaselee, garrisoned the Summer Palace.

Plate 7. French Transport. The transport was, in fact, Mongolian camels.

Plate 8. German Four-in-Hand Brake. This carriage was brought to Peking from Berlin.

MILITARY OPERATIONS

Plate 9. R.I.M.S. *Dalhousie*. This Royal Indian Mail Ship, named for a former governor-general of India, took Lieutenant Steel to Shanghai and Hong Kong in October 1901.

Plate 10. Taku North Fort, April 1901. This fort, captured the previous June, was now guarded by Italian and British marines.

Plate 11. The Sewer Gate. This entry point enabled General Gaselee's forces to reach the Peking legations.

Plate 12. Bamboo Ramp. This structure had been built by the Chinese to emplace guns on the wall of the Imperial City. (Official photograph.)

Plate 13. Ruins. This photograph shows the ruins of the Legation Quarter after the siege. (Official photograph.)

Plate 14. Breach in Wall. This is a view of a cut in the south wall of the Chinese City for a new railway into Peking. (Official photograph.)

Plate 15. "Puffing Billy." This shunting engine was constructed by a royal engineer out of a stationary engine and a "truck." (Official photograph.)

Plate 16. Curios. These collected curios were reported by Lieutenant Steel to have been returned to the Chinese. (Official photograph.)

OFFICIALS AND INDIVIDUALS

Plate 17. Li Hung-chang. The seventy-year-old governor-general at Canton, who had abstained from supporting the Boxers, was the acceptable, obvious negotiator to settle the peace.

Plate 18. Lt. Cdr. Roger Keyes. Keyes distinguished himself at the Taku forts in 1900 and later became Admiral of the Fleet Lord Keyes, G.C.B., I.C.V.O., D.S.O. He died in 1945.

Plate 19. Gen. Sir Alfred Gaselee. Gaselee commanded the British contingent of the allied relief expedition.

Plate 20. Field Marshal Count von Waldersee. He is reviewing British troops on January 1, 1901, in the south court of the Forbidden City. (Official photograph.)

Plate 21. Gen. O'Moore Creagh. The general, who commanded British forces at Shanghai, is posed with his wife and aide.

Plate 22. Chinese Servant and Dog. Lieutenant Steel merely identified this charming pair as "Liu and dog."

Plate 23. Maj. T. E. Scott. D.S.O. Scott, here wearing a mourning band for Queen Victoria, was identified as the "first man into Peking."

Plate 24. General Barrow. Barrow, here shown with two of his staff, one an Indian, served as provost marshal of Peking during the occupation.

THE CHINESE

Plate 25. Wood Sawyers. These men were employed by the British to build barracks.

Plate 26. A Barber. He is posed with his mobile "shop."

Plate 27. Neighbors. These Chinese lived close to Lieutenant Steel.

Plate 28. Workers. These men worked in a Peking cloisonné factory.

Plate 29. A Funeral. This is a forlorn winter scene in a Peking street.

Plate 30. A Storyteller. This was a familiar type of Peking street entertainer.

Plate 31. Prisoners. They are wearing the traditional device for holding and humiliating prisoners, the cangue.

Plate 32. A Peking Cart. The vehicle has extended axles for lines to assist in hauling it through muddy stretches.

THE CITY OF PEKING

Plate 33. Drum Tower. Lieutenant Steel enjoyed riding to this spot. (Official photograph.)

Plate 34. Pei T'ang Cathedral. The Roman Catholic cathedral was successfully defended throughout the siege. (Official photograph.)

Plate 35. Coal Hill. Coal Hill, or Mei Shan, stood in the center, north of the Imperial City, overlooking the Forbidden City. (Official photograph.)

Plate 36. Lama Temple. This temple in the northeast of the Tartar City was another favorite destination for Lieutenant Steel while he was riding. (Official photograph.)

Plate 37. The Tsungli Yamen. This structure housed China's prototype foreign office. (Official photograph.)

Plate 38. Forbidden City. Upon relief of the siege, allied troops, principally Americans, entered the Forbidden City. (Official photograph.)

Plate 39. Marble Boat. This is said to have been the empress's response to the demand for expenditures for a modern navy. (Official photograph.)

Plate 40. Throne of China. This symbolic site of imperial Chinese authority sat dolefully empty during the time of the allied occupation of Peking.

4

Consolidation of Peking, Looting, and Chasing the Boxers, August 15–September 28, 1900

15 August Wednesday The Americans and Japanese got a footing inside the Imperial City after losing somewhat heavily (Captain Reilly, USA, killed), and we took the Imperial Carriage Park next door. We are utilizing it for barracks for our troops. The imperial carriages, harness, etc., all gilded, are a very curious sight, especially with drabies sleeping inside.

I went up with Sir Alfred to the top of the Ch'ien Men and had a fine view of the whole place [Plate 13]. One can scarcely see the north gates from the south—it is so far. I went out into the Board of War with Dering and shot some pigeons for dinner and saw some ghastly sights, dead Chinese. We found a lot of Mauser ammunition. The sniping becomes less and less every hour.

The Americans I watched some time, lying in wait at the end of each street and shooting every Chinese that showed his head. The Japs and Russians hold the eastern and part of the northern sides. The Americans and ourselves, part of the southern sides of the Tartar City. Everyone is gradually converging on the Imperial City.

16 Thursday I could not go out all day, owing to a boil on the leg which was spreading and becoming very painful. The different Powers are all scrambling for the Imperial City, soldiers of all nationalities looting everywhere. We have just started a Prize Committee, and all stuff brought in is put into the fund [Plate 16]. A small silver store was found and brought in sacks containing silver ingots of a peculiar shape called "shoes," about £2000 or £3000 worth.

The state of dirt and filth in the Legations could hardly be exaggerated, sanitary arrangements practically nil. Just outside dead Chinamen lie unburied for days. The missionary station of Peitang was relived today by a mixed force of all nationalities [Plate 34]. Everyone seems on the loot, the French, Japanese, and Russians having got a good start of us.

17 Friday I had to stay in all day in my dirty corner of a dirty pavilion with a very painful boil on the leg. The whole of the Tartar City is gradually being absorbed by the different Powers and the Chinese driven out. The only place unoccupied seems to be the Imperial Palace or Forbidden City, international guards being placed all round its gates. Reports state that all inside have committed suicide. The stores, etc., from the boats and rations arrived today, a most welcome relief. My Chinese servant engaged yesterday bolted.

18 Saturday Stayed in nearly all day and went in evening to the south gate of the Chinese City (which is held by two guns of the 12th Field Battery Royal Artillery and some infantry) with Sir Alfred, as there are reports of a large gathering of the enemy in the Imperial Hunting Park. Patrols of the 1st Bengal Lancers found cavalry and infantry of the enemy in scattered bodies.

19 Sunday George Barrow arrived in morning. Rode in evening with Colonel O'Sullivan to the "Coal Hill," north of the Imperial City [Plate 35]. Heard a looting party of marines was going to

Prince Kung's house and went with them along a road *horrible* with Chinese corpses in all stages of decomposition and was nearly sick. Kung's palace is a perfect wonder of wealth, and we carried away any amount of treasure for the common fund. [Prince Kung, the Hsien-feng emperor's brother, had come to power with the empress dowager, negotiated with the Europeans in 1858, and directed China's foreign affairs until 1884.]

20 Monday Everything is quieting down in the Chinese and Tartar Cities. George Barrow has been appointed Chief of Police in one quarter of the Chinese town [Plate 24]. I went with him in the morning round his new domain and saw a great many Chinese Mohammedans who *now* are very anxious to oblige. Formerly they were among the most rabid antiforeigners. Was sent by General Barrow with Keyes to arrest a blackmailer named Cook, who has been making a good business out of various Chinese merchants by promising them protection of the British flag. Had quite an amusing little adventure with him. A reconnaissance south of the Chinese City became engaged with some Boxers, the guns taking tea with them. The Boxers seem to have quite nonplussed 1st Bengal Lancers' horses with their long spears!

21 Tuesday Spend whole morning getting the horse lines into order and collecting forage for the horses. Moved my own kit from in front of the Legation to a tent in the Imperial Carriage Park, to be near the horses. Rode in afternoon on a Chinese pony, which I have annexed, with the General, Keyes, and General Barrow to the east gate of the Chinese City, where we came in first. Here the Naval Brigade are encamped on the wall. The naval officers there say that it was explained to them by Chinese that the cause of the little resistance to us was the premature Russian and Japanese attack on the right. All troops defending the east gate and Chinese City were withdrawn to the east wall of the Tartar City, the taotai [specifically, in Chinese, an "intendant of circuit," but, loosely, an "official"] of this portion of the Chinese City committing suicide when he found we had done him in the eye. Rained heavily at night.

22 Wednesday Went out with Sir Alfred and General Barrow to the southwest corner of the Tartar City, where the 1st Sikhs are. The officers are all in a splendid house, very clean and sumptuously furnished, and the men are almost as well off. The southwest is by far the best part of the city I have seen yet, being almost free from smells, open and full of fine houses, presumably the property of mandarins and high officials. On the way we (unfortunately for them) came across some officers of the Chinese Reg't. doing a bit of looting with carts, etc., and the General was naturally somewhat angry. This will now mean that anything got by officers and not handed over to the Prize Committee will have to be declared. Very hard on some of us who have only a few odd things.

23 Thursday I had intended to go right round the walls of the Tartar City today, but Ryder, who was coming with me, could not go, so I stayed in. The convoy with a great many women and children left early in the morning for Tungchou, whence they go down to Tientsin by junks. The Legation is gradually being emptied of all the refugees, etc., and is being cleaned up by gangs of Chinese coolies. I visited the houses on the west of the Legation, mostly burned, from which the Chinese used to pour in rifle fire. The number of empty cartridge cases and military rubbish of all kinds was immense. I went in the evening with Sir Alfred to the Temple of Heaven, and whilst he was talking to Colonel Tipping, went and saw the Temple, a most lovely place, surrounded by groves of fir trees. I saw Cheyne and Jock Rose there.

24 Friday Went out early with all the horses to exercise, down through the Ch'ien Men toward the Temple of Heaven. Went out after breakfast with Keyes to the "Coal Hill," north of the Imperial City. Climbed up to the top and got a magnificent view of the whole of Peking, including the Forbidden City or Imperial Palace, with its yellow-tiled roofs. Got a good view, too, of the Summer Palace and hills to the west and north. Went on into the Russian camp and bought fifty dollars worth of silver bars from the soldiers there. Went with the General in the evening to the "Coal Hill" and round back by the west of the Imperial City home and dined with Sir Claude and Lady MacDonald.

25 Saturday, 26 Sunday Went to the Communion Service in the Legation Chapel at 9 a.m. In the afternoon went with Sir Alfred and General Barrow to call on the Americans at the Temple of Agriculture, Harper [General Chaffee's aide-de-camp] asked me to dine on Tuesday. Two of the 24th Punjab Infantry sepoys [native Indian soldiers] were shot in a street row by Americans, a most unfortunate business.

27 Monday Went with Boyce Kup (the General's Chinese interpreter) to our portion of the Tartar City, southwest, in the morning and brought away two cartloads of fine grain (millet and black beans) and some bran from a grain seller's shop for the Headquarters Staff horses. The horses seem to do very well on the millet, which I am giving unground and unsoaked, but I have to soak the black beans.

    The afternoon I went again to the southwest quarter to a Prince's palace and with some trouble caught a deer, which however the sowars unfortunately killed coming back. Got a Chinese pug dog there, too, rather a nice little brute. The house was full of splendid furs, etc., which unfortunately one couldn't take owing to the strict orders anent looting. A triumphal entry into the Forbidden City by representatives of all arms of various Powers is arranged for tomorrow morning.

28 Tuesday Paraded at 7 a.m., each corps and department furnishing a representative party in front of the south gate of the Imperial City. The Russians and Japs each, eight hundred; ourselves, Americans, four hundred. The Russians entered first, then Japs, then ourselves, Americans, French, Germans, and Austrians, and marched straight thro' to north gate near "Coal Hill." The 12th Field Battery Royal Artillery fired the salute of twenty-one guns. Many high officials were found inside, very sullen and sick looking [Plate 38].

When the march was completed, the staffs and various rag-tag and bobtail, newspapermen, etc., came back, and we were shown thro' the more public parts of the Palace. The Russian officers and correspondents did a certain amount of looting, as is their habit, rather poor form from an English point of view.

The various parts of the Palace are splendid in the actual buildings, but are grass-grown and have the indescribable appearance of combined splendour and neglect so common to Chinese palaces [Plate 40]. I talked with one of the mandarins who spoke English and one who spoke French well, the Secretary of the Tsungli Yamen [China's Foreign Affairs Office]. They were both very interesting and have been to Europe several times. One of them said he would send me a pony(!), but I doubt whether he meant it.

29 Wednesday Rained all morning. I went in evening with Sir Alfred to the Temple of Heaven. Two Italian naval officers dined with us and stayed till very late. Rather a business, talking so long in a mixture of broken English and if possible worse French.

30 Thursday Wrote letters all the morning, and it rained pretty heavily, and no one got out much. Sir Walter Hillier arrived with an escort of the 16th Bengal Lancers from Tientsin. Sir Claude MacDonald got me the pony that the mandarin in the Palace promised me, a fine sturdy grey, about 13 hands—1. Lunched with Wray of the Marines after going round all the east part of the defences with him and Norreys, the chaplain, a most interesting ramble among ruined houses, barricades, Chinese shelters, and all sorts of rubbish. A mail bag arrived.

31 Friday Rained off and on all morning. Tried several places to get the horses under shelter, with no avail, but in the end got a good place at the north of the Legations. Went out on my new pony as far as the Temple of Heaven and found him no go, cataract in both eyes.

1 September Saturday Sir Alfred went out to the west, to the junction of the rail towards the Western Hills, with General Barrow, Sir Walter Hillier, and Pell. I stayed in and moved the horses under cover into a "Tonga" behind the Legations. [A *tonga* was a light, two-wheeled vehicle drawn by a pony. The term was often used to designate an ambulance, but here Lieutenant Steel seems to use the word to indicate a sheltering horse stall.]

2 Sunday Went to the service in the Legation Chapel at 11 and in the afternoon rode to the Lama Temple, in the northeast part of the Tartar City, and the Drum Tower, both most interesting places [Plates 33 and 36]. An English mail arrived in the evening.

3 Monday Went out soon after breakfast with Boyce Kup down to our southwest corner of the Tartar City and out with Colonel Pollock and a party of the 1st Sikhs to two Prince's palaces. There we collected a good deal of warm clothing for syces, grooms, and servants. [A *syce* is a groom.] The whole of both places had been ransacked, and a lot of Chinese had broken into the first the night before and had bagged a huge store of rice. Lunched with the 1st Sikhs in their house, a splendid place, full of beautiful furniture, etc. Heard Prince Ch'ing had been escorted in by a party of the 1st Bengal Lancers and Jap cavalry. [The moderate Prince Ch'ing had been replaced by the pro-Boxer Prince Tuan on June 10, 1900. He was to return as plenipotentiary to negotiate peace terms in 1901.] Sir Walter Hillier left in the morning for Tungchou.

4 Tuesday Got up early and went with the horses and a lot of mules and carts to one of the palaces we visited yesterday. Loaded up with dried fodder and bran and returned and worked at the stables. The General Pell went to visit the big Lama Temple I saw on Sunday afternoon. I bought several things at the auction in the evening for Lord Curzon, cloisonné and bronze. Wrote to Baker-Carr and Addie. A convoy with the remaining women and children left in the morning early for Tungchou and Tientsin. General Fukushima lunched with us. General Barrow made a tour of inspection with a committee of the Allies of places suitable for barracks.

5 Wednesday Went out after breakfast with Sir Alfred round the Japanese lines north of the Tartar City and outside it, out of the Te Sheng Men and in at the An Ting Men. Had refreshments with the Japanese brigadier commanding their 21st Brigade and found one officer who talked a little German.

6 Thursday Went out early with Dering of the Legation to the southwest Tartar City to the Palace of the Princes. It has been sacked and looted and very little remains except china, which may be good, but scarcely anybody knows anything about it. We shot some pigeons there.

7 Friday Went out early to the same palace as yesterday and got some china and trifing curios. Arranged to get a lot of china up for anybody to take who likes. A mail came in, with Shanghai papers of the 22nd with news of the entry into Peking in them. Went to the auction in the evening and bought some cloisonné, etc., for the Viceroy. Admiral Alexieff, commanding the Russian Fleet, arrived yesterday and returned General Gaselee's call of this morning.

8 Saturday, 9 Sunday Went to Parade Service at 8 a.m. Went with General Gaselee to call on General Wilson. [Maj. Gen. James H. Wilson, although senior to General Chaffee, arrived as his second-in-command. He subsequently led the U.S. forces in pursuing Boxer remnants in the countryside.]

10 Monday Started at 7 a.m. with Colonel O'Sullivan for Tungchou, with our convoy. I took a box that I had packed for the Viceroy (bronzes and cloisonné) which Boyce Kup is to take for me to Sinho. We followed the "American road," which runs just south of the canal all the way. It poured in torrents as we started and again at Tungchou, and I got soaked thro'. Major Scott, [Plate 23] 3rd Sikhs, and Hill, of the Chinese Reg't., put us up and did us very well. The road was fearfully bad, knee deep in mud in places. Saw Boyce Kup off for Tientsin in a junk and was very glad I wasn't going, as all the shelter he had was a few masts.

11 Tuesday A fine bright day after the rain, and everything very clear and lovely, the hills beyond Tungchou being very plain and blue. Started at 7:30 a.m. and came back along the road we advanced along on the 14th (very bad), with two sowars of the 1st Bengal Lancers. Got in to Peking at 11:30, having trotted most of the way, about fifteen miles. Went to the American Mission in the Yu Wang Fu and bought a couple of sheepskin coats. Went in afternoon with the General to the southwest corner, and out at the hole in the wall which the sappers have made during the last week. The turf outside along the wall is perfect, and we had a good canter. Visited a place there which is going to be used for a hospital, a brand new building, very fine indeed.

12 Wednesday Went down to the Temple of Heaven and paid bills for shoeing. Went round to all commanding officers at General Gaselee's orders. Got my things I had bought from the American Mission.

13 Thursday 9 a.m. went with Pell and Keyes to the Lama Temple in the Imperial City and got some boxes for kit in some houses close to—and came back about 1. In evening went with Sir Alfred to call on the German general, who was, however, out. Went on to the 1st Sikhs to tea. Lady MacDonald was there too. They (1st Sikhs) have a very good "bundobust" [Anglo-Indian term meaning "arrangements"] all round and are very comfortable. In my opinion by far the smartest regiment out here. They have started all kinds of shows, farmyard, etc., etc. The Lama Temple this morning very interesting, usual lofty, dark building containing splendid bronzes and a library which, I believe, is priceless.

14 Friday Was feeling very seedy yesterday evening and up all night, but better today, tho' rather warm. Kept to my quarters most of the day. Sent off a letter and money order for the faithful Algoo, who has been with me three years now thro' various experiences. Sold two-thirds of the silver I had for $140, great bunnia [Indian term for a shopkeeper who guarantees transactions] business.

Generals Chaffee and Wilson (Amer.) dined.

15 Saturday Went down to Temple of Heaven in afternoon and saw the hockey which has just been started. Went round and had a look all round the Temple, parts I hadn't seen. Heard of the fearful gunpowder accident at Tungchou, twenty men killed and many injured. Hill (Chinese Reg't.) badly injured. [Hill had been Lieutenant Steel's host on September 10.]

17 Monday Went out with Sir Alfred, Phillipps, Pell, and Keyes, starting at 6 a.m. with a German force, going out to the Western Hills to cooperate with the British and American force (under General Wilson) which started yesterday to surprise the Boxers in a stronghold in the hills. We arrived too late, as the British and Americans had got there at 6 a.m. and surprised the Boxers, killing fifty and occupying the valley in which the seven temples (occupied by Boxers) are. I counted thirteen dead Boxers myself. We explored the temples and pagoda and returned with the German force to Peking, fourteen miles in the afternoon. I have not seen any place in China yet to compare with the beauty of this valley. General Dorward arrived from Tientsin. Our force remained out and will stay four days Boxer-hunting.

18 Tuesday Keyes left early by convoy to return to this ship. I went down to the Temple of Heaven after breakfast, taking General Barrow's horse to the vet. There are several cases of glanders down there and rinderpest. Saw Major Steele and arranged for coolies to clear the Legation stables. Heard of poor Hill's death at Tungchou, from effects of the fearful powder accident on the 14th (twenty-eight men died from it). Rode with Sir Alfred and General Dorward to the southwest Tartar City and looked at palace selected for hospital, etc. Dined with Lady MacDonald and arranged for pony to carry Poole out tomorrow.

19 Wednesday Worked at the stables most of the morning. The Punjab Coolie corps—I will guarantee to do less work in more time than any other body of men. Rode through the Russian quarter in afternoon with General Barrow, O'Sullivan, and Phillipps to look at the observatory, bronze instruments on the east wall of the Tartar City I have never seen any bronzes to touch them yet, and the instruments are quite wonderful, a bit knocked about by shot and shell, but in wonderful preservation.

A mail arrived just before we went out.

I took all the horses outside the Tartar City this morning and had a canter on beautiful green turf, thanks to our new gate or hole in the wall.

J.G. Scott lunched today (in charge Shan States?).

20 Thursday Went out on Brinks directly after breakfast to find General Linevitch (commanding Russians) with an important letter from Sir Alfred. Was quite wrong in my first direction and found the Headquarters eventually near the "Coal Hill." I tried to come back west side of Imperial City inside, but got into a cul-de-sac and had to come all the way back. It rained in torrents last night, making everything very muddy and beastly today. Was introduced to Towers, the new First Secretary.

21 Friday Took all the horses out beyond the west wall before breakfast and gave them a trot on the turf and back through the German, north gate of the Chinese City and back through the German quarter. The Headquarters mess were photographed by a Jap photographer. Polo was started down at the Temple of Heaven—chukkers both for Chinese and Indian ponies. I did not play as there is a virulent outbreak of glanders down there, and it isn't good enough risking ponies.

22 Saturday Sir Claude and Lady MacDonald came back from Palichow. I went with Dering's gun to the moat outside west wall by our new gate and saw two snipe and shot one, not a very brilliant morning's work. Brinks not at all good to look at, swellings under jaw, etc., and discharge. Segregated him. Went for a walk with Colonel O'Sullivan along wall of Tartar City to Ha Ta Men and back and looked at the captured guns.

24 Monday Went early with the Hyderabad Cavalry duffadar to the new gate of southwest Tartar City. Left our horses with the guard and walked up to the moat outisde. Put up about ten snipe, *very* wild. Killed two and a couple of snippets and returned rather pleased. I used the remainder of my cartridges to polish off some of the dogs in the Legation, great foul brutes that wander in starving from the city. General Richardson, commanding Cavalry Brigade, came up to lunch. I went down in afternoon to the Temple of Heaven and saw the 16th Bengal Lancers, who arrived yesterday, and Teed, 14th Bengal Lancers, Fane, Grimston, etc. The General decided to go to Tientsin tomorrow, and I am to go to Hong Kong with Low on Friday to get stores, etc. My breeches arrived from Hammond's.

25 Tuesday Went down with Sir Alfred to inspect the 16th Bengal Lancers at the Temple of Heaven. They ranked past in single file, horses a bit fine drawn, but the regiment looks very fit. Went on down the lines of both 1st Bengal Lancers and 16th Bengal Lancers. The 16th compare very favourably with the 1st. Teed, of the 14th Bengal Lancers, came up to lunch and Sir Alfred and Colonel O'Sullivan left for Tientsin at 1:30. I went with Craik, 19th Bengal Lancers, and Sarel, 11th Bengal Lancers, and Teed to an auction in the French quarter by the Italians. Everything too expensive, so didn't buy. Coming back, met Paddock, of the U.S. Cavalry, and took him back to tea and gave him a pair of breeches(!), of which he was in want. Very windy and cold all day with dust storm.

26 Wednesday Getting quite cold, especially morning and evening. Arranged with Low that we do not start till Saturday. General Richardson, commanding Cavalry Brigade, came to lunch and Grimson and Troup. Saw Fairfax, of the Durham Light Infantry, who is with the Chinese Regiment, and he gave us an account of the fearful accident at Tungchou on the 14th.

27 Thursday Went down in one of the Dhanjiboy's [probably the name of a contractor for transport] tongas to the Temple of

Heaven in the evening to a gymkhana and had a very jolly time. Many Americans and several of other nationalities turned up, and the events were fairly full up. It is getting quite cold, and I was glad to wear a thick coat all day. Arranged about starting on Saturday for Hong Kong.

5

A Trip Out to Other Parts of China, September 29–November 20, 1900

29 September Saturday Started at 8 a.m. with Low, Stoddart, and Douglas for Tungchou, with the convoy. Got there about 1:30 and got all our kit at once into a light, small boat, with a sort of rough cabin. We laid in some supplies and started. We have with us five men of the 26th Baluchis and Nasrullah, my orderly, and are taking boxes, etc., for a good many people, mostly furs, china, etc., that fellows are sending home.

1 October Monday Going down river, got to Yangtsun at about 12. The Russians have repaired the railway bridge and have repaired the line, it is said, some two kilometers to the north. Saw the General's boat waiting for him at Yangtsun and met Sergeant Stringell with a junk full of the officers' Headquarters Staff kit and got my portmanteau from him. The railway has been completed some time to Yangtsun, and daily trains are running. Sir Alfred and O'Sullivan had been to Tientsin to see the C-in-C, Count von Waldersee, and were returning to go out with the Peking part of the Expedition to Paotingfu, which is contemplated. [Field Marshall Count Alfred von Waldersee had missed out on the glory of the march to Peking, but had now arrived, at the Kaiser's insistence, to be the supreme commander. Plate 20] We saw an immense quantity of duck on flooded land and reached Sinku.

2 Tuesday Started very early from Sinku, reaching Tientsin at about 7:30. Sent off our luggage under escort of our sepoys in a lighter down the river. Breakfasted with Major Bond, who put us up for the night. Heard we were to sail in Royal Indian Mail Ship *Dalhousie*. Lunched with Marshall (doctor of 17th Bengal Lancers, who has a field hospital here). Went out in afternoon to the camp of the 20th Punjab Infantry and had a long talk with Colonel Woon. Tientsin has changed very much since we left it. Full of foreign troops, and any amount of Chinese have come back and everything is very busy. Heard accounts of capture of Peitang Forts, where Russians forestalled us, and rumours of H.M.S. *Pigmy* having taken Shanhaikuan, which we hope are true.

3 Wednesday Started 9 a.m. for Sinho in train, reaching there about 11. Lunched with Napier, Central India Horse, who is commanding there, and got off down the river at about 5:30 p.m. so as to get the flood tide over the river in a dirty little steamer run by Japanese, the *Kikaku*. Reached the Fleet about 8:30 p.m. Stopped to allow two naval officers to get on board H.M.S. *Endymion* and got on board *Dalhousie* about 9 [Plate 9]. Engaged a servant.

4 Thursday Started from the Fleet at daylight and steamed somewhat slowly so as to reach Chefoo at daylight tomorrow. The *Dalhousie* is taking Major Penrose, Royal Engineers; Creagh, 4th Punjab Infantry; and Barton, Political Officer, to Weihaiwei. We have with us an old subadar of 1st Sikhs returning to Kohat to go on pension. [A *subadar* was a chief native officer of a native company.] It is a delightful thing to be on such a smart, clean ship after the dirty old *Lebenghla*. The latter is to be paid off we hear, but had just gone up to Shanhaikuan. We saw Guy, the chief officer in Tientsin, a first rate chap who deserves a better billet.

5 Friday Arrived at Chefoo and landed before breakfast with and for mail, with the Captain.

Bigger place than I expected, any number of Chinese stores selling European goods. Picturesque place, surrounded by hills and a grotesque Chinese wall running up and down hill for miles, "to keep out the smallpox." Only stayed a couple of hours. Arrived at Weihaiwei about noon. Creagh and Major Penrose, Royal Engineers, disembarked, and a nursing sister and a sick gunner arrived on board for Hong Kong. Left Weihaiwei about 5 p.m.

8 Monday Anchored off Shanghai in river. Very chilly, rainy day. Stayed on board all morning and went off in rain with Low to call on Gen. Sir Garret O'Moore Creagh. [Plate 21. General Creagh later succeeded General Gaselee.] After lunch saw Watson and Stewart. Returned and went on shore again with Captain Kendall and did some shopping. Very cold and beastly in driving rain. Dined on board.

9 Tuesday Started down river at 9:30 and had a fearfully narrow squeak of a collision with a big German steamer coming up—had to run aground to escape—but got clear very quickly. Enroute Hong Kong.

13 Saturday Arrived Hong Kong early. Landed and reported arrival at Staff Office. Went and placed my two orders with Messrs. Lane and Crawford.

14 Sunday Went in evening with Captain of *Dalhousie* to the "Happy Valley" [the Hong Kong racecourse].

15 Monday Hong Kong. Spent day in shopping, etc. Met "Gran" Turner and Norman, who are here on remount duty. Dined with 22nd Boroda Infantry at Kowloon, with Colonel Baillie, who was second-in-command of 20th Boroda Infantry when I was in them.

20 Saturday Left Hong Kong early morning and got it fairly rough outside.

25 Thursday Arrived at Shanghai about noon and heard there that the *Dalhousie* is to go back to Bombay at once and that we shall have to tranship everything into the transport *Lalpoora,* which arrives this afternoon. Went out and saw Stewart and Crawford and did some shopping in Shanghai with Low.

28 Sunday Started from the wharf at Shanghai about 12. Found that the Mussulman havildar [a native noncommissioned officer], Hong Kong Reg't., in charge of guard on stores, had broken into a case of liquor and was made prisoner. Anchored at Woosung waiting for telegraph cable we are taking board.

29 Monday Started from Woosung early in morning, towing a lighter. After a short time the hawsers parted, and it delayed us some time picking the lighter up again. We have to go very slow on account of the lighter, a great nuisance. Fairly foul all day. Set to work in the afternoon to mend the worst of the cases of stores which were smashed.

30 Tuesday Took the evidence about the case of theft from the stores, which meant a good deal of hard lying on the part of the Hong Kong Regiment sepoys. Fine till about 5 p.m., when it began to rain hard. At 9:30, as it was beginning to blow, the

Captain decided to take the crew off the lighter, which delayed us some time.

2 Friday Weihaiwei. Woke up to find it almost calm. Got a bad sore throat. Got in to Weihaiwei about 3:30 p.m. and anchored. Went ashore with Low and saw General Dorward. Creagh came on board, and Low and I went off and dined with him at the "club." Met Keyes and Gee, doctor of the 5th Bengal Lancers.

3 Saturday Weihaiwei. Went ashore about 11 a.m. and took a photograph or two. Lunched with Keyes, who commands H.M.S. *Fame* (destroyer), and had a most interesting look round. Took two photos of Brady and Keyes and the officers of the little ship. Went on shore, the *Fame* sailing for Shanghai at 3 with the *Goliath* and *Taku* (the destroyer the *Fame* captured from the Chinese at Taku on the 14th of June). Walked up to the signalling station on the island of Liukungtao.

4 Sunday Went on shore and walked to the end of the island with Low and Creagh, 4th Punjab Infantry, and saw ruins of the old Chinese casemates. Went over to the mainland, Weihaiwei, and saw the new hotel they are using as hospital and had tea in Chinese Reg't. mess and came back in a sampan (sailing) after taking some photos.

8 Thursday Arrived at Sinho about 7 a.m. and decided to go by river to Tientsin, leaving the lighter and stores to be towed up. Saw Napier, who has made a fine place out of the desert at Sinho! Got to Tientsin about 2:30, and I went over to the 20th Punjab Infantry and got put up.

9 Friday The lighter arrived above 12. It was *bitterly* cold and a hurricane of dust blowing, and Low and I had a very miserable time unloading the lighter and getting part of the stores on junks.

Got my English and other letters for the past month. Saw General Barrow, who is on his way up the Shanhaikuan line.

12 Monday Gave evidence in the case of the Hong Kong Reg't. havildar and got permission to start and made all preparations for an early start tomorrow. Got a very nice note from the 20th Punjab Infantry, with whom I am staying and for whom I brought up stores from Hong Kong, asking me to consider myself a guest of the Reg't. during my stay here. Very jolly seeing all of the 20th, Colonel Woon, and others with whom we were (13th Bengal Lancers) in the Mohmand expedition.

13 Tuesday Started at about 10 a.m. in our junk, but were hopelessly blocked by a crowd of junks by the French bridge of boats and did not really make a start till 12. Pulled up all afternoon and arrived about 6 p.m. (quite dark) at Peitsang, where we have a post. Got Hutchinson, who commands the post, and Picton, Royal Engineers, to come and dine on board. We made ourselves pretty snug with the stove, but it was freezing hard outside. We have five junks loaded with our stores with us, about twenty-six men of different regiments on board.

14 Wednesday Started early and had a difficult job ploughing thro' floating ice of which the river is full. Saw any amount of duck, easy shots, and longed for a gun. Stalked some with my Mauser pistol on the water, but naturally didn't hit them. Had to tie up to the bank as a dust storm came on, and it was impossible to go on. Later on the wind went down a bit, and we fetched up below the bridge at Yangtsun for the night.

16 Friday Passed Tsaitsun early in the morning. Any amount of floating ice in the river, which melted as the day went on. Passed a lot of junks going down with Chinese on board, mostly flying the Japanese flag. Got to Hosiwu about 2 and went on, doing about six or eight miles on the way to Matou, and tied up to the bank for the night.

17 Saturday Reached Matou in the evening after a long day sticking on mud banks every now and then. Saw a Chinaman who had been captured with arms taken out to be shot. Wogan Brown of the 3rd Boroda Cavalry came to dinner with us on the junk. Stayed at Matou for the night.

20 Tuesday Got some carts and sent off 110 boxes and hope to get off tomorrow. Rigby arrived from Tientsin. A bad dust storm all morning and bitter cold wind. Sergeant Stringel and my syce and Brinks arrived in afternoon. Low and I went and dined with Major Scott, 1st Sikhs, and officers of the post.

6

A Winter in Garrison in Peking and the Summer Palace, November 21, 1900–March 27, 1901

21 November Wednesday Got rest of our kit packed on carts and marched to Peking, arriving there about 2 p.m. Found the General and Headquarters established in a very nice house in the Imperial City. Have got very comfortable quarters in a little courtyard all to myself.

22 Thursday Went in morning to the German sports and race out on the old racecourse, east of Chinese City, and saw the Field Marshal Count von Waldersee for the first time.

23 Friday Got my riding school made and began getting my room to rights and comfortable. Walked with Pell and Sir Alfred to the Imperial Palace and German Headquarters to see Colonel Grierson, who is on the Field Marshal's staff. Pell and I were entertained by Count Eulenberg, an apoplectic officer of Hussars, fourteen stone and peg top thighs, the very cut of a German horseman.

24 Saturday Went down to the Temple of Agriculture and dined with Harper, the American aide-de-camp, at their Headquarters.

Phillipps, Pell, two German officers, and I were the guests. Not a very elevating entertainment, except so far as the effect of mixed liquors on the American and German officers went.

25 Sunday Went to service with Sir Alfred at the Legation Chapel in morning and afterwards to lunch with George Barrow, who is Police Commandant, Chinese City, and is living in a series of very interesting old temples.

26 Monday Peking. Had all the horses out at 7:30 a.m., very brisk and cold, and gave them a real good warming up in my new manège. Went for a walk with Sir Alfred in afternoon to the Ha Ta Men. General Barrow came back from Tientsin yesterday.

27 Tuesday Peking. Got all horses into their new stables and am sacking the five useless sowars who have been nominally getting in forage, but actually amassing wealth by "sodagiri" [black-marketing] and doing nothing.

28 Wednesday Rode down in morning with Sir Alfred to the Chinese City and saw George Barrow at his "yamen," dispensing justice as Police Magistrate. Saw one Boxer who was just going to be shot, but had to promenade with a placard first setting forth his crimes. Went round to south gate of the Chinese City and looked at the gap in the wall thro' which the railway is being brought [Plate 14]. Came home in a piercing north wind. Li Hung-chang came to call on Sir Alfred in afternoon, and I got home to stand a second for a photo which turned out very good. [Li Hung-chang, the prominent diplomat, was governor-general of Kwangtung at the outbreak of the siege. With Prince Ch'ing, he was judged acceptable to the powers for conducting the 1901 peace negotiations. Plate 17.]

29 Thursday Got a good deal done with the stables, syces' houses, and clothing, etc., in the morning. Wilson Johnston, 24th

Punjab Infantry, brother of the one I was with at Rugby, came to lunch, and we had a long talk over the old school, etc. Went down to the water southwest of the Forbidden City and tried to skate, but the dust was too thick on the ice. (Partially taught a Pathan of the guard to slide, but he came tremendous howlers, which rather damped his ardour.)

30 Friday Peking. Rode down thro' the southwest corner of the Tartar City in morning and saw the 12th Field Battery Royal Artillery New South Wales Naval Brigade in their winter quarters in the "Chang Wong Fu." Rode on to the new hospital and saw Major Johnston, 12th Field Battery, who is ill and then on to Sir Norman Stewart and the Headquarters, 1st Brigade, all very comfortable and snug in an old palace. Went in afternoon to the same piece of ice with Colonel O'Sullivan, Phillipps, and a lot of the escort and had great sport teaching them to slide. My Chinese coolie I had before going to Hong Kong came back, much to his own delight and indeed mine. He is worth ten Indian servants.

1 December Saturday Worked all morning getting stables, riding school, and the escort of the 16th Bengal Lancers into proper order and took Sir Alfred round to see them. Drew my pay and went to lunch with Whittall, Reuter's correspondent, who is living in a Chinese house in the Italian quarter. Rode with Colonel O'Sullivan after into the Japanese quarter, as far as east gate.

4 Tuesday Went with Sir Alfred in morning to the Japanese quarter, which is *crowded* with Chinese booths and shops selling furs, curios, etc., at extraordinary prices [Plates 25 through 32].

5 Wednesday Went with Sir Alfred, General Barrow, and most of the staff to the funeral of Colonel Yorck von Wartenburg in the Imperial Winter Palace. Very cold, standing listening to funeral oration by German pastor. Great many officers of all nations present, and the streets were lined by German soldiers. Dick, 2nd Punjab Infantry, arrived in afternoon and is staying with us.

6 Thursday Went down by myself, walking, to the Temple of Heaven to lunch with Fane and General Richardson, etc. Heard Fane's burlesque read over, in which we are all to perform after Xmas and walked back with the General to the Legation after lunch. Dr. Morrison, special correspondent of the *Times,* and Kinder, of the Railway, dined in Headquarters Staff mess. Field Marshal Count von Waldersee came to call on the General.

7 Friday Printed some photos in morning and went with Dick to the Jap quarter, where we bought some furs. Very cold and blowing a blizzard all day. Mrs. Conger, Miss Conger, Miss Pearce, and Mrs. Rockhill of the American Legation came to tea in the mess. [The Conger ladies had suffered through the Boxer siege with U.S. minister Edwin Conger. The new U.S. minister, William W. Rockhill, was a most distinguished scholar of China, Mongolia, and Tibet. He had been instrumental, with the Englishman Alfred E. Hippisley, in the formulation of U.S. Secretary of State John Hay's Open Door notes on China in September 1899.]

11 Tuesday Went down to see the 12th Field Battery Royal Artillery in morning. Heard Oldham is likely to go back to his battery in India. Left my camera box to be made up by the collar maker. Went in afternoon to call for Sir Alfred at the Austrian Legation and went to call at the American Minister's. Saw Mrs. and Miss Conger, who gave me tea, very hospitable and nice people, and met Mr. and Mrs. Rockhill (also Americans).

   The first engine since the reconstruction of the railway came up today and went back to Tientsin [Plate 15].

12 Wednesday Rode out with Sir Alfred and General Pipon, Royal Artillery, to the Nanhaitze (Imperial Hunting Park) south of the Chinese City, a grand open plain covered with grass. Returned about 1 p.m. Saw the site of the new railway station at the Temple of Heaven. Went out with my Chinese servant, shopping in the afternoon.

13 Thursday Rode Brinks round by the Drum Tower in morning and bought a delightful, hand-painted book up there. Major Scott, Post Commandant at Tungchou, came up and arrived in time for luncheon, and we were all very glad to see him. Walked with Sir Alfred in afternoon as far as the Sun Chih Men (southwest gate of the Tartar City).

17 Monday Went all round the Summer Palace (which we in conjunction with the Italians are now garrisoning) and took some photos [Plate 6]. It gives one the impression of the fairy palace of children's books, very fantastic, picturesque, *and* childish. The great lake was fairly frozen over, and we had some pretty good skating, tho' the dust spoils it. Came in in the afternoon, taking about three hours to ride in on my Chinese pony. Dined with the Congers at the American Legation, where there was a great crowd of American officers, mostly 6th Cavalry, and had a very pleasant evening and came away very taken with the simple, homely hospitality and cheeriness of the Americans.

20 Thursday Went out with Sir Alfred and nearly all the Headquarters Staff, starting 9:30 a.m. to the Hunting Park, about three miles south of Chinese City, to witness firing by guns of 12th Field Battery Royal Artillery; two naval twelve-pounders, manned by Australian bluejackets [Plate 4]; and an American field battery. It came on suddenly intensely cold, and I came back about 3 p.m., thoroughly chilled, and went to bed.

26 Wednesday Went over to lunch and out for a short time with Pell and spent evening developing photos, which turned out very good of Summer Palace, etc.

29 Saturday Hutchison and Wilson Johnston lunched. I was not allowed to go down again by the doctor to second performance of the burlesque, so went for a walk instead, in Japanese quarter with the subadar of the guard. Sir Alfred has been ill in bed four days with a very severe cold.

31 Monday Attended rehearsal of tomorrow's parade in morning and went down in a tonga to the final performance of the burlesque at the Temple of Heaven in the afternoon. Low and Jermyn lunched with me. Arranged to go out to the Summer Palace on Wednesday and wrote to Major Du Boulay, asking him if he would let me be a member of his mess.

1 January 1901 Tuesday Peking with China Expeditionary Force. Parade of all troops in garrison in front of the Imperial Palace and march past Field Marshal Count von Waldersee, present representing the German Emperor. Troops present: 12th Field Battery Royal Artillery, Australian Naval Brigade, 7th Rajputs, 24th Punjab Infantry, 26th Baluchis, 1st Sikhs, and sappers, and marines. The General and Headquarters Staff gave a luncheon party at the International Club to commemorate the opening of the Federation Parliament to the Australian officers. Sir Alfred was unable to be present as, tho' better, he was still confined to his room after an attack of influenza.

5 Saturday Walked up with Pell to the Pagoda Hill, west of the "Coal Hill," and got a magnificent view of the whole of Peking under snow and also mountains to the northwest and north. Took one photo of "Coal Hill." Went out after lunch with Pell to the Japanese quarter of the Tartar City and bought a lot of game, etc.

6 Sunday Went out in a tonga with Pell and Colonel Bond for the day to the Summer Palace and made arrangements for the proposed visit of ten days or so that the General is going to make in order to recruit after influenza.

7 Monday Peking. Rode down to the Temple of Heaven in morning to look at a horse of Satel's for Napier at Sinho, then round thro' Chinese City (German quarter) and in to the Tartar City by the Sun Chih Men. Went to the 24th Punjab Infantry and gunners. Colonel Grierson lunched. I went by myself to the Library and shot some pigeons. A Chinese deputation, with an umbrella and various presents from villages south of the Chinese City, waited on Sir Alfred and said how pleased they had been at their treatment by native troops!

8 Tuesday Sold my Chinese pony "John" to Ker of the British Legation for $100. Went with Pell to the Japanese quarter and bought provisions, etc., and decided to go out to the Summer Palace tomorrow.

9 Wednesday Summer Palace, Peking. Went out in a tonga to the Summer Palace and took out in carts the stores, etc., for our stay there. Went out with Moorhead (who was doctor of the 16th Bengal Lancers) to look for duck round the lake, but had no luck.

11 Friday Went out for a walk round the Summer Palace with Sir Alfred in the morning and skated in the evening on a piece of ice cleared from snow on the lake in the afternoon. The whole of the lake in front of the Summer Palace is covered with snow, except at the mouth of the canal where the water comes in where it is warm and does not freeze.

14 Monday Went out with Wilson Johnston before breakfast to circumvent duck. Shot two mallard, which however fell on unsafe ice and were eaten by a brute of a fox by the time we tried to get them in afternoon. Sir Alfred, Major Du Boulay, Campbell of The Guides, Pell, and I lunched with the Italian officers here. (The Italians hold the Summer Palace in conjunction with us.) An awful ordeal—talked bad French for three hours and ate and drank horrors. Went after the duck again in evening, but only got one teal.

15 Tuesday Skated in the morning on the lake beyond the island in which the Emperor was confined during the "coup d'état." [Steel refers to the seizure of the Kuang-hsü emperor by the empress dowager, his incarceration, and the end of the Hundred Days of Reform on September 21, 1898.] The ice was splendid. Sir Alfred came out and skated, and after a bit we got an improvised sledge and took him up and down. Went out with Wilson Johnston in the evening after duck, but they have become very wild and scarce and we got nothing.

16 Wednesday Went out with Major Du Boulay, Pell, Gattrell, the Chinese interpreter, and Wilson Johnston to an old, practically-deserted palace on the hills west of this, five miles, taking twenty sepoys. Found that a great deal of the furniture of the Summer Palace had been taken and stored there. We brought back some copper plaques off an old temple roof, thickly gold plated, to see what they are worth. Had a very interesting day and took a photo of a fine arch covered with beautiful, glazed tiles. Very cold and cloudy.

18 Friday Came out again in the morning and went out in the evening with Moorhead and Campbell and got some grand shots at duck during the evening flight, bagging five. Campbell got two. The difficulty is getting them out of the canal, which is free of ice owing to warm springs. The whole of the Italian officers came over and dined with us, and we had a most amusing evening and a great concert afterwards and did not get to bed till very late.

21 Monday Pell, Campbell, and Gattrell went out to the old ruined palace in the hills we visited on the 16th and brought in a great many of gilt tiles from a roof. They are said to be valuable—as well as some furniture. I skated with Sir Alfred on the rinks which we had cleared of snow which fell last night. The whole of the good ice on the lake is spoilt by the snow.

22 Tuesday Peking. Sir Alfred, Pell, and I came back to Peking in the morning. Had a wire before leaving Summer Palace to say that Colonel O'Sullivan had broken his leg (thigh), slipping over some steps near the mess—a clean break luckily, but it will take some two months to mend. Conran and Berger (latter Hong Kong Reg't.) are staying with us.

23 Wednesday Went round to the Bank and Legation in the morning and with Dick to see Miss Smith in afternoon. Bought some furs and curios for Lord Curzon and made arrangements to see some more. Pringle came up to see Sir Alfred—wants to apply for Staff Corps.

24 Thursday A Reuters telegram announced the sad news of the death of our Most Gracious Majesty the Queen. Every nation represented here sent senior officers to Sir Alfred during the day, and the Field Marshal Count von Waldersee came in person.

27 Sunday Went to service held in the square south of the Forbidden City to commemorate the anniversary of the Emperor of Germany's birthday. All representatives of the Allies present, and a great many of the German troops marched past the Field Marshal afterwards. Rode in evening out of east gate of the Tartar City round the north side and in at west gate, a long round of about twelve miles.

28 Monday Went with several other fellows to visit the Imperial Palace or Forbidden City, where one can only go in a party under permit from one of the generals. Saw a great deal more of the palace than when we marched thro' last August, including the private apartments of the Emperor and Empress Dowager crammed with all sorts of incongruous European toys—harmoniums, clocks, pianos, clockwork toys, etc. [Plate 40]. Went in afternoon with General Barrow down to the book sellers' quarter in the Chinese City and met Prince Chi'ng's private secretary, who was very affable and assisted us buying curios, etc.

29 Tuesday Went out on Brinks in morning up to the Italian headquarters with a card for Sir Alfred to Colonel Gallioni and back by the German Headquarters. Asked von Lettow to come out and shoot, but he is off on an expedition, Wildberg and Kötwitz coming instead. Low and Wilson Johnston lunched, and W.J. and I rode up after lunch with a couple of sowars to the northeast corner of the Tartar City and on the moat outside the wall. We found a piece of very good ice and had some capital skating. Heard of tragedy at the "Hotel du Nord." Dening of 3rd Boroda Cavalry shot by man who killed his wife and committed suicide. Dening in Legation badly wounded.

30 Wednesday Went over to the Legation in morning and saw Hewlett and borrowed some books for Colonel O'Sullivan, who is doing very well. Saw Griffiths and arranged to take him out to Summer Palace tomorrow instead of Wildberg and Kötwitz, who can't come. Went in the afternoon to the Field Marshal's with notices about the parade to be held on Saturday, with funeral service (the day of the Queen's funeral). Saw General von Schwartzhof, the Chief of Staff, and then went down to General von Strotha in the Chinese City.

31 Thursday Went out in a tonga to the Summer Palace (taking Griffiths and Cowie, Royal Engineers, with me) to shoot. Found lots of duck, but they were very wild, and we only got four teal

E. R.

Head-Quarters, British Contingent, China Field Force.
Peking, 30th January, 1901.

The following British Field Force Order is circulated for the information of those who may wish to attend the Military Funeral Service in memory of Her Majesty Queen Victoria.

No official invitations will be issued, but places will be reserved for officers of the Allied Forces; military detachments; members of the Diplomatic and Consular Services and civilians, that may be present.

There will be a Parade of all troops in garrison at noon on Saturday, the 2nd February, in the Court-yard, in front of the South entrance to the "Forbidden City," at which the Burial Service will be read for our late beloved and lamented Sovereign, Queen Victoria. 101 minute guns will be fired by 12th Battery, Royal Field Artillery, from 11 a.m.

At 11-55 the Massed Pipers of the 1st Brigade will play a "Lament."

At noon the Burial Service will be read by the Chaplain, during which the troops will "rest on their arms reversed," after which the Royal Salute will be given by order of the General Officer Commanding 1st Brigade, on this command the Pipers will play another dirge, which will be followed by "The Last Post."

The troops will then shoulder arms, after which they will march to quarters.

Dress.—Full dress.

By Order,

E. G. BARROW, Major-General,
Chief of Staff, B.C., C.F.F.

and two mallard. Saw there Colonel Alexander, Napier, and several fellows of the 24th Punjab Infantry. Took a couple of photos of one of the bronze dragons for the Royal Engineer fellows and came back in one and one-half hours, the paved road being free from ice and very good going. The sun is getting quite strong, and it is not dark till 6:15. A little snow in the morning and bitterly cold after coming back in the tonga.

2 Saturday Grand Parade in front of south gate of Forbidden City at 12 Noon. Funeral Service. All Allies represented by detachments of many officers. Walked over to the Field Marshal's quarters in afternoon with Pell and asked Kötwitz and Waldmann to come out on Tuesday to the Summer Palace for a shoot.

5 Tuesday Went out by tonga to the Summer Palace, taking two German officers—Waldmann, a Feldjäger, and Kötwitz, a naval officer—to shoot. The duck were very few and fearfully wild and we got nothing. Tried to sail the ice yacht in afternoon, but there was not enough wind and so we skated a bit.

7 Thursday Commander Nicholson of H.M.S. *Phoenix,* which is frozen in the Pei Ho at Sinho, and Alston, Royal Navy, and McSwinery, 7th Dragoon Guards, called in morning. Mrs. Willis and Mrs. Ker, British Legation, came to lunch. Saw Eulenburg and Kötwitz, the former driving (very well) four-in-hand [Plate 8], in afternoon and arranged to go out with Kötwitz tomorrow.

11 Monday Got room ready for Rose and St. John. They arrived by the train in the afternoon from Tientsin. Whittall came over and gave me the photos he had got printed for me in Shanghai. Blowing hard—north wind and dust very disagreeable all day.

13 Wednesday Rose and I went to lunch with Colonel Grierson at the Field Marshal's quarters. Colonel G. is on the F.M.'s staff. Luncheon was in the German officer's mess room. Saw Eulenberg and heard that Kötwitz had a very bad fever indeed and fear it is enteric. Sir Ernest Satow came over to see Colonel Grierson whilst we were there, and we walked back to Headquarters together. [Satow had succeeded Sir Claude MacDonald as British minister.]

14 Thursday Rose, St. John, and I went out to the Summer Palace, taking Vernery, of the Chasseurs d'Afrique, and Picquot, of the French artillery. Picquot and I rode, the others going in a tonga. We walked all round, the place being even more wantonly destroyed than when I last saw it, and had lunch in one of the rooms we were using first as a hospital. Very cold and a very high wind. I rode Brinks, who is very above himself, and came back by the north gate and Drum Tower.

17 Sunday Very much milder. Lunched with von Lettow at the German Headquarters and took a lot of photos there. Came back with the Graf von Eulenberg in their four-in-hand, which E. drives very well. Called with Sir Alfred on Mrs. Whittall and Mrs. Squiers. [Mrs. Squiers's husband, First Secretary Herbert Squiers of the U.S. legation and a fifteen-year cavalry veteran, had been a hero of the siege.] Jock Rose and St. John left today. Major Gebsattell dined.

18 Monday Went and called on Colonel Shiba at his house opposite our Legation. [Lieutenant Colonel Shiba, the Japanese military attaché, had been considered by all the outstanding military leader in the defense of the legations.] Rode down to the Jap quarter to get some things for the General. Drew my pay and got a draft on Cook's at the bank. Rode down outside the Tartar City wall to the 1st Sikhs and saw the earthwork for the new French railway line from Paotingfu in course of construction. An "Armée Befehl" has been issued by the Field Marshal, announcing that owing to the demands of the Powers not being complied with, troops are to hold themselves in readiness for renewed operations end of this month.

19 Tuesday Chinese New Year. Rode before breakfast out at the hole in the wall (or Great British gate!) to the Tartar City west and right round the outside of the Chinese City across country to the south gate of the Chinese City. Von Lettow lunched with me, and we compared the price, etc., of uniforms in the German Army with ours after. I got a lot of information regarding their accoutrements and kit generally, which seem to me to be for the most part not nearly so practical and good as ours. Count von Eulenberg came round in his brake and four-in-hand, which he manages astoundingly well over the worst roads in Asia.

21 Thursday, 22 Friday Went again to the Forbidden City, this time with General Campbell and young Elles. Took a good many photos and, wandering about, lost the others and came back via the north gate of the Palace. Sun very warm in middle of day, but it freezes at night, all night. Colonel Shiba of the Jap Army, who was so prominent during the defence of the Legations and whom I had met in India, came and lunched with me. He is rather keen on buying my bay Arab, Brinks. Walked with Phillipps and Dick and Bingley down to the Railway Station in the afternoon and dined at the Legation with Sir Ernest Satow and Sir Walter Hillier.

23 Saturday Packed some curios for Sir Alfred all morning and got a new exercising course made for our horses. Took Brinks over to Shiba, where a rum-looking little bunder of a Jap vet cocked his head on one side and crabbed the finest Arab he's seen in his life. Played football in the tournament for Headquarters Staff.

25 Monday Went down to the cemetery outside southwest Tartar City to represent Sir Alfred at Dr. Dudgeon's funeral, an old ex-missionary who had been long in China, thro' the Siege, and who had been employed superintending the conservancy and cleaning up of the Legation after the Siege. Prendergast and Barwell, 4th Punjab Infantry, and Major Barrett and Colonel Pollock, 1st Sikhs, to lunch. I rode down over very bad roads on General Barrow's bike, as a novel sensation, to the football outside southwest wall of Tartar City. General Campbell and young Elles went back to Tientsin. Very much warmer and sun quite hot.

27 Wednesday Sold Colonel Shiba of the Japanese Army my bay Arab pony Brinks for $500 and bought a Mongolian pony of his for $50 and rode said beast down to see the football matches in afternoon. Very windy and dusty all day. Arranged to go to the German dentist on Friday, 2:30.

28 Thursday Lunched with Griffith, Royal Engineers, and took some photos and went afterwards and shot pigeons at the south gate of Forbidden City. Sir Alfred gave a big dinner at the International Club to F.M. Count von Waldersee and other notables. The pipes of the 26th Baluchis played, and I got over their Khaltak company and arranged a Khaltak dance after dinner which was a fizzing success.

1 March Friday Rode early before breakfast on my new pony round southeast corner of Chinese City, along east wall, and in at Ha Ta Men. Very bitterly cold, windy, and dusty. Lunched with Colonel Grierson at the Headquarters Staff mess of the Germans and went round and was operated on by the German military dentist after. Walked with Sir Alfred out at Ha Ta Men, which the Germans are pulling down, and in at east gate of the Tartar City.

2 Saturday Went out after breakfast, taking Nasrullah and a sowar of the escort to the Imperial Hunting Park. Saw no deer at all after riding a long way. The Germans and others have fairly scared them away. Returned about 4 p.m. The Australian Naval Brigade officers from the Lama Temple detachment dined with us, as well as Major Boulanger and Menzies, Chinese Regiment.

4 Monday Went after breakfast to the quarters of the Chasseurs d'Afrique, and Guichard, who is commanding the troops, had them out by the "Coal Hill" [Plate 35]. I took four photographs of them, which I returned home and developed and they turned out excellent. Saw a good deal of the sample drill, etc., and was much impressed by their smartness and "go." They have very nice stocky little Arabs all entires [stallions]. Went down after lunch to see the final of the football between the 24th Punjab Infantry and 1st Sikhs, won by former. Met a great many French officers that I know there and Masturci and the doctor of the Italians. Wynne (Aust.) and Pratt (Reuter's) came to tea at my place, and I dined with Ryder at the Intelligence mess.

5 Tuesday Went to Hong Kong and Shanghai Bank and sent pay for Feb. to Cook's. Panet and Bessine, the two French officers I met the other day, came and lunched with me. Sir Alfred, Phillipps, Dick, and I went walking up in the Japanese quarter buying curios in afternoon. Arranged for dinner Pell and I are giving tomorrow at International Club. Very much warmer, and no wind—only 5 degrees of frost last night and thermometer at 41 at 10 a.m.

6 Wednesday General Gaselee saw a last parade of the New South Wales Naval Brigade as they are soon to go back to Australia, their places being taken by the half-battalion, Royal Welch Fusiliers, from Hong Kong. Dick and I rode over to the Palais Rotond and lunched with Colonel D'Espérey and Beynaguet, of the 21st Chasseurs, and met a great many French officers, some of them old friends, Panet and Bessine among others. I took some photos there. Heard of the Russian private treaty or agreement with China re Manchuria, which excites general indignation. Pell and I gave a dinner at the International Club with German officers we know and who have been very hospitable to us. Phillipps and Dick came too and Count Eulenberg. Count von Königsmark, von Rauch, von Lettow, Waldmann, and Wildberg were the guests.

7 Thursday, 8 Friday, 9 Saturday Went with Sir Alfred to the reinterment of the bodies of those who died or were killed during the Siege of the Legations. They were buried at first in the British Legation grounds. The 12th Field Battery Royal Artillery furnished carriages for the coffins (fourteen) and the Australian contingent, and a squad of 16th Bengal Lancers formed the escort. Bitter cold, very dusty.

11 Monday Sir Alfred and Pell left by the 8:40 train for Tientsin. Sir Alfred intends making a tour of Tientsin, Tongshan, Shanhaikuan, and possibly Weihaiwei and Shanghai. I finished up with the dentist and went down in afternoon to the funeral of Captain Paddock, 6th U.S. Cavalry, at the American camp. Dined with Manifold at the Royal Australian Headquarters mess. Guichard, of the Chaseurs d'Afrique, lunched with me.

12 Tuesday Went to the dentist for the last time and paid him ($200) £20, but the relief is quite worth the money. Went down to lunch with General Stewart and Staff, 1st Brigade, and took a photo of them. Went round afterwards on General Barrow's bike (very rough going) to 1st Sikhs and 24th Punjab Infantry and down thro' the Sun Chih Men into the Chinese City and home by the Ch'ien Men. Saw the first train on the French, Peking-Paotingfu Railway, which has got up to the terminus near the Ch'ien Men, inside Chinese City and along outside of the Tartar City wall.

13 Wednesday Went to the International Committee for the Administration of Peking, of which I am to be the British member, vice Selwyn, who is going on two months' sick leave. Went down walking in afternoon to the gunners at Chang Wang Fu, but found no one in and on to Selwyn in order to take over papers and get some information as to the work of the Committee. Colonel MacDonald, just arrived from Tientsin, came and dined.

14 Thursday Rode Pell's pony early before breakfast out west gate Tartar City and in at Ch'ien Men. Worked most of morning at translation of German Committee meeting proceedings. Reeves, U.S. Attaché at the American Legation, and Rigby lunched with us. Colonel MacDonald, Director of Railways, Valentine Chirol ("Times"), Colonel Tullock, and Backhouse dined with us. [Here Lieutenant Steel meets the famed sinologist Edmund Backhouse, a scholar of undoubted talent, but certainly an eccentric and most probably a forger of documents.] Railway Staff office is wanted at Yangtsun. General Barrow is debating whether to send me temporarily, during Sir Alfred's absence on tour.

15 Friday Went out early before breakfast riding Pell's pony with Whittall, Reuter's correspondent, who rode my Mongolian pony. We got out as far as the Race Course, which is about three miles west of the Tartar City wall. Went down after breakfast and took photos of the 24th Punjab Infantry and developed ones I took the other day at the French luncheon. Went out for a walk in afternoon with Phillipps thro' the Legation and met and talked to Tower and Porter. General Barrow and Dick went to see General Voyron. The French have been misbehaving in Tientsin and caused unpleasantness. Serious question on with Russians over a disputed piece of railway land at Tientsin.

18 Monday Rode Pell's pony out to the Race Course before breakfast, taking Nasrullah on my Mongolian pony. Came back along the south wall of the Tartar City, where the French Railway now runs. Went round to Hong Kong and Shanghai Bank about Administration Committee money. Porter and Hewlett, two of the students at the British Legation, lunched with me. Colonel D'Espérey and Lieutenant Ferradini dined with us.

20 Wednesday Temple of Heaven before breakfast with General Barrow. Rode to see Du Boulay after lunch and on to the Temple of Heaven. Saw General Richardson and Angelo, etc. Went over to Beasley after dinner. Fifty Australians went down to Tientsin from here and the Hong Kong Reg't. from railway line—on account of the Russian complication over the siding at Tientsin. General Baillou (French) from Paotingfu went down by morning train to settle the difficulties which have arisen thro' French soldiers misbehaving in Tientsin. More satisfactory telegrams arrived after dinner—things quieting down in Tientsin.

22 Friday Went down to the Temple of Heaven on Pell's pony and General Barrow's mare. Lunched with Sir Walter Hillier and Mrs. Hillier, the former got me up some good embroideries to see, of which I bought $80 for Arthur [Steel's younger brother, later Sir Arthur Steel-Maitland, Bart., M.P.].

Dined with Rigby at the Intelligence Dep't. mess. Met Napier, who has been special service officer up the Yangtze. The trouble at Tientsin with Russians is coming to an end, both sides agreeing to withdraw their guards.

23 Saturday Went down to the Temple of Heaven as usual, training. Bought $100 worth more of embroidery for Arthur and others and cashed his cheque $144. Went down to see Major Du Boulay, on business, in morning. General van Schwartzhof, Chief of German Staff, Major von Marshall, Herr von Mummer (German Minister), and Richthofen, Attaché, dined with us.

24 Sunday Rode out on General Barrow's bicycle to the Summer Palace, out along the canal bank and in by paved road. General Barrow and Phillipps went in a tonga. Had a sail on the lake, perfectly splendid weather.

26 Tuesday Went down to see the New South Wales contingent, Naval Brigade, off at the station at the Temple of Heaven. They are going back to Australia. Breakfasted with George Barrow and went after lunch with Major Everitt and Hill of the R.W.F. to Chang Wang Fu. Saw Major Johnstone and the Germans and returned via the Winter Palace. Colonel Radford and Stirling of 4th Punjab Infantry, from Shanhaikuan, have arrived and are staying with us.

7

Lieutenant Steel Departs from China, March 28–April 28, 1901

28 March Thursday Very windy and much colder in morning, so did not go down to the course as usual. Feeling very seedy, liver or something, all day—worse than usual. Went down and saw Grimston in afternoon.

29 Friday Saw Manifold in morning and got him to vet me. He is going to put me on a regular course and recommends me to go home, if possible to Carlsbad. Went out for a change to the Summer Palace with Norie and Rennie Tailyour. We are putting up in a nice clean house on the ridge of the hill overlooking the lake. Went out with Norie to shoot in the evening, there being a quantity of duck and geese about. Norie got a goose and I a duck.

30 Saturday Went out with Norie and Rennie Tailyour to the Yüan Ming Yüan, or Old Summer Palace, about one mile from the new one. This was the place destroyed by us in '60 and is now a wonderful maze of waterways and ruins. I shot two snipe there. We went out in the evening after duck, Rigby having joined our party.

REGULATIONS

FOR

VISITORS TO THE "SUMMER PALACE."

Frequent complaints having been made that articles of furniture, etc., are removed from the "Summer Palace" and damage caused to the buildings by the carelessness of visitors—the following regulations regarding the admission of visitors have been framed by the Commanders of the Italian and British Forces.

1. The Palace will be open only on Sundays and Thursdays between 11 a.m. and 4 p.m.

2. Officers of the Allied Forces, and soldiers, who must be accompanied by an officer of their contingent, members of Diplomatic the Corps and civilians, shall be allowed to visit the "Summer Palace" if in possession of a written permission, signed either by one of the Commanders of the Allied Forces, or by one of the Ministers, as regards individuals attached to their respective legations or *personally* known to them. On the pass, which must be presented on arrival to the Commander of the British or Italian Detachment at the "Summer Palace," should be noted the name of the senior officer and number of persons authorized to accompany him.

3. The "Summer Palace" will be open for H.E. Field Marshal Count von Waldersee, the Commanders and General Officers of the Allied Forces, Ministers of the Diplomatic Corps and guests invited to accompany them, by delivering their card in person to the Officer Commanding British or Italian Detachments at the "Summer Palace" on any day of the week between 11 a.m. and 4 p.m.

4. Visitors shall enter the Palace by the gate guarded by British troops and leave it by the same gate or by the north-west gate, guarded by Italian troops

5. Visitors are forbidden to enter the rooms or buildings occupied by British or Italian troops or those which have been closed by order.

6. During the hours above specified, British and Italian non-commissioned officers will be present in order to accompany parties of visitors through the buildings which are under the protection of their respective Contingents.

7. Visitors are earnestly requested not to damage or remove anything from the Palace, and to abstain from smoking in the buildings as, already, one of the pagodas has been partly burnt through carelessness.

(Sd.) **A. GASELEE**, Lieut.-General,
Commanding British Contingent,
China Field Force.

(Sd.) **GARIONI**, Colonel,
Commanding Italian Contingent,
China Field Force.

PEKING, 22nd MARCH, 1901.

Printed at the "Queeen's Own" Madras Sappers and Miners Field Press.

1 April Monday Went down early to the Temple of Heaven and saw Manifold again after breakfast. He says I ought to go home at once and so have made up my mind to it. Went down and saw to pitching a camp for the General and Staff down at the Temple of Heaven.

4 Thursday Went down before breakfast, the only time one can get decent fresh air, to the Temple of Heaven with Whittall. [He refers to the dusty atmosphere of Peking, as March and April winds blow in from the Gobi Desert.] Went round to the Hong Kong and Shanghai Bank after breakfast. Down to Railway Station in afternoon to meet Sir Alfred and Pell, who returned from their tour to Shanghai today. Sold Wingate, 14th Bengal Lancers, my tent and camp bed.

8 Monday Went with Sir Alfred, General Barrow, Phillipps, Dick, Jim Turner, and Sir Pratab Singh to call on Field Marshal Count von Waldersee, as it is his birthday and everyone was there from all contingents. Went with Sir Alfred in the afternoon to the Nanhaitze, or Imperial Hunting Park, south of the Chinese City to the German races, which were very childish and dull.

9 Tuesday Went to the meeting of the International Committee for the Administration of Peking and afterwards appeared before the medical board. Asked for six months, but they said it was not enough and made it a year. Very windy and dusty and disagreeable. Struck off duty from today.

11 Thursday Went out for a short walk in morning and got Sir Alfred some china spoons, etc., that he wanted. Very bright and pleasant early, and then in afternoon there was a dust haze obscuring everything in a yellow fog. Stayed in all afternoon and finished some packing of things for the Viceroy. Decided to go down to Tientsin on Sunday and wired to Ray, Deputy Assistant Adjutant General there, asking him to put me up. Today was the first day of the assault at arms, and all the others went down with Generals Gaselee and Barrow.

13 Saturday The others went down to the last day of the Race Meeting, which was, I believe, very good. Got the Viceroy's boxes, etc., down to the Station and said goodbye to Norie, Rennie Tailyour, Rigby, and others. Gough, 1st Sikhs, and two naval officers dined and are staying here.

14 Sunday Started for Tientsin by train, Colonel O'Sullivan coming to see me off. Madam O'Gorman, wife of Col., The O'Gorman at Hong Kong, came down on same train. Put up at General Lorne Campbell's house at Tientsin, their mess being Colonel Swan, Assistant Adjutant General; Ray, Deputy Assistant Adjutant General; and Watling, Orderly Officer.

15 Monday Went to Jardine, Matheson and Co. and arranged and paid for my passage and handed over four boxes for the Viceroy to be sent to Calcutta, as well as two of my own, one for London and the other for Calcutta (saddle). Arranged for my three servants going back to India. Lunched with Creagh at the Astor House Hotel and saw Nye, the dentist, in the afternoon.

Dined at Mr. Cousins', the head of J.M.'s firm in Tientsin, and Baron Gunsberg (of the Russian Secret Service) as well as Doughty, of the Royal Welch Fusiliers.

16 Tuesday Got my kit packed, paid up my servants and took them over to the Native Base Depot and booked my passage to Shanghai by one of the "China Merchant" ships. Went down by the afternoon train to Tongku, where Dunsterville, of the 20th Punjab Infantry, is Railway Staff officer. Went down river in a sampan to the *Sinyu,* got my kit on board and dined early by myself. Made friends with Li Hung-chang's son, who is also going to Shanghai with his cousin to bring his mother up. Later on two employees (Germans) of the Russo-Chinese Bank at Port Arthur came on board and Poore, an officer of the U.S. ship *Monocacy*, who is going home. Had a most interesting conversation (all in French).

17 Wednesday The ship not sailing till tonight, I went after breakfast with Poore to see the North and Northwest Forts at the mouth of the Pei Ho. The Northwest Fort is held by our marines and Italians and the north one, by Japs. Took some photos and met a couple of our Marine officers. Went after lunch with Poore to say goodbye to Dunsterville at Tongku Station. Poore moved into my cabin, as we have got to double up and the ship is full of foreigners—two Germans, two Trappist fathers, a French captain, etc., etc.

Madame O'Gorman and Lady Brownrigg turned up, among a crowd of other passengers, and we sailed about 11 p.m.

18 Thursday After a wretched, cold day arrived at Chefoo at 6 p.m. and got rid of a part of the passengers with whom we were very overcrowded. Miserable little tub of a steamer and very bad waiting, etc., (Chinese boys). Got away from Chefoo about 9 p.m.—cold, raining, and generally dismal.

19 Friday Very disgusting all day, rounded the Shantung promontory about daybreak and came into a heavy cross roll, which lasted all day and made everyone sick, including my cabin companion, Poore, of the U.S. Navy! Went to bed at 6 p.m. Ate nothing all day and lay awake clutching the side of my berth all night.

20 Saturday Smoother and going southwest. Hope to get in tonight. Arrived at Woosung about 3 p.m. and got alongside the wharf in drizzling rain at Shanghai at about 4. Went to the Astor House Hotel, a very well got up place and very comfortable rooms. Went down in a ricksha in the rain and saw Stewart, D.A.A.G.

21 Sunday Went to see General and Mrs. O.M. Creagh [Plate 21] at their house and lunched with Stewart and the others of the 2nd Brigade Staff. Seeing Shanghai at a disadvantage, gloomy weather and drizzle, but a place beautifully kept and gardens, etc., lovely. Saw Mrs. Stockley, wife of Colonel S., 16th Bengal Lancers.

22 Monday Astor House Hotel, Shanghai. Went and saw about my passage at Jardine's. Heard General Barrow's going to England indefinitely postponed. Lunched with General and Mrs. Creagh and went round to E.W.O. [romanized Chinese name for Jardine, Matheson and Company] and saw Madame O'Gorman, who had some sketchy ideas about going up to see the tidal bore at Hangchow, or to Ningpo. Dined at the Hotel at same table as Mrs. Stockley and husband.

23 Tuesday Went down thro' the French concession and to the city of Shanghai with Madame O'Gorman, walking the city, which is weird, picturesque, filthy to a degree. Major Scott, 3rd Sikhs, who is also going home, arrived from Taku. I went down to Stewart's to take tea and dined with General Creagh, a tête-a-tête dinner, as Mrs. Creagh was away at a concert. Enjoyed my evening very much.

25 Thursday Took my kit to the Peninsular and Orient office and sent it off to Cook, London; developed my photos at a Chinese photographer's and saw Scott for a moment.

Got a wire from Arthur announcing his intended marriage on July 10th.

Went in afternoon to call on H.M.S. *Astraea* and afterwards to see Ivy, the dentist, and had a most expensive gold crown fitted to a tooth! Went to Kahu and Komor's, the Japanese shop, the only place worth going to in the East for curios. Bought a tea service as a wedding present for Arthur, the most beautiful thing of its kind I have ever seen.

27 Saturday Shanghai. Breakfasted at the Staff Mess, went to the mooring in the launch, and got on board the *Empress of India*. Stewart came down with us on the launch to see Major Scott and self off, and we started at 4:30 p.m., down the Yangtze River. Have got a cabin to myself as far as Yokohama, but if crowded after that shall go in with Sir Walter Hillier.